ONE MINUTE TO MIDNIGHT

CLOSING OF THE CURTAINS ON PLANET EARTH

Garfield O. Daley

© **Copyright 2020 by Garfield Daley**

ISBN:978-1-949343-96-0

All Rights Reserved.

No part of this publication may be reproduced, stored in an electronic system, or transmitted, in any form or by any means, electronic, mechanical, photocopying or otherwise without the prior written permission of the author.

To order by phone: 1-772-777-1022 (International)

WhatsApp: 1-876-833-7631

Email: info@endtimebook.net

Internet: www.endtimebook.net

DEDICATION

This book is dedicated to the memory of my late Pastor, Bishop Stanford J. Grizzle, who through the years had given all of himself in ministering the Word of God in such a deep and profound way. The notes compiled in this presentation have their roots in Bible studies that he has taught me over the years.

Through the years his pastoral leadership impacted me to the point where I was determined to follow him as he followed Christ. His leadership was exemplary, his care was gentle and far-reaching, and his love for the people of God knew no boundaries.

A genuine man of a Great God. Thank you, my Pastor.

ACKNOWLEDGEMENT

One Minute to Midnight would not have come into existence without the inspiration of the Holy Ghost. I give honour to the Great God of heaven who allowed me the wherewithal to put this together. It is in Him that I live, move and have my being, and I am forever indebted to the Almighty.

Sincere thanks to my beloved and faithful wife for her unswerving devotion and rock-solid support as I undertook this project. Her calm and unflinching patience, and being my number one cheerleader, have contributed in no small way to the inspiration for doing this work. God gave me the best, and she continues to be a sterling and comforting companion, even after thirty years together.

To Jewel and Crystal, whose no-nonsense approach to the project's execution ensured they reviewed the manuscript from the first draft. Jewel, for the order and flow of the chapters, and Crystal for the title of the book.

To John-Mark, who gave the final nod of approval. Without that sanction, the book could not be released. You guys are awesome!

This book could not be published without the sacrifice, patience and expertise of the following individuals:

- Kerry-Ann Barrett
- Gary Gordon
- Tracy Lewis
- Kerri-Ann Palmer
- Erica Redman

They were the core of the editorial team and selflessly helped in the coordination, typing and arranging of this work.

Anthony Harrison, Andrew Martin and others assisted in content review and gave pertinent advice—I thank you.

On the technical side, I acknowledge Mark Harrison, Czyzon Robinson, and the entire technical support arm.

Magnificent job team! My deepest appreciation to all...

PREFACE

The subject of the end times and the events leading up to the return of the Lord, have generated a lot of discussion by saved and unsaved alike. Signs of the end of times and prophecies relating to these signs have been the main focus in many of these discussions. These pages in no way give an in-depth study on the subject but provide a basic understanding of where we are with respect to the coming of the Lord Jesus Christ.

It is my desire that this book will serve to impress upon us just how close we are to the Saviour's coming and help us to be ready and waiting.

The four horsemen of Revelation 6 and their significance will be reviewed. The mark of the beast will be revealed. The role of the New Age Movement and the New World Order will be explored. The prophecy of Daniel's 70 weeks will be broken down. The momentous occasion of the rapture will be explained, and the requirements to get ready and stay ready for the return of our Saviour, Jesus Christ, to take his Bride (the Church) away, will be outlined.

Changing world structures, human relations, diseases and epidemics, and even nature itself are harbingers for the imminent return of Jesus. This book seeks to make us aware of the happenings and to help us to prepare. It is "One Minute to Midnight" and the curtains of planet earth are closing.

I leave you with the refrain from the Chicago Mass Choir, which is a simple, earnest wish that we will all be ready. We want to be ready against that day, when we will boldly and happily declare "Behold He cometh! Behold He is here!"

I Pray We'll Be Ready—Chicago Mass Choir
I pray we'll all be ready
I pray that we'll all be ready
I pray we'll all be ready
For His return
I pray that we'll get our business straight
So we can all meet at the gate
I pray we'll all be ready for his return

I pray that we'll all, be ready
I pray that we'll all be ready
I pray that we'll all be ready
For His return
I pray that we'll give our hearts a search
So that we won't be playing church
I pray we'll all be ready for his return

I pray that we'll all, be ready
I pray that we'll all be ready
I pray that we'll all be ready
For his return
I pray that we'll get down on our knees
So the Lord can wash us clean
I pray we'll all be ready for his return

TABLE OF CONTENTS

	PAGE
Dedication	iii
Acknowledgement	iv
Preface	vi
Introduction	1
Chapter 1 - Chaos (The Future)	9
Chapter 2 - The Horsemen are Coming!	32
Chapter 3 - That Terrible Mark – 666	58
Chapter 4 - One World Religion and the New Age Movement	85
Chapter 5 - End Time Calendar (Daniel 70 Weeks)	97
Chapter 6 - The Rapture	116
Chapter 7 - Armageddon	133
Chapter 8 - Getting Ready or Ready Waiting?	148
Chapter 9 - Questions & Answers	160
Glossary	174
Bibliography	175

INTRODUCTION
(A look into the future)

The "end of days" has been spoken about since the early church and anticipated by most religious groups. It was Peter, who stood up after the Pentecost experience, and preached a profound message that 3,000 people responded to in its eternally saving grace.

He quoted the Prophet Joel in his timely discourse:

> **"It will come about after this that I will pour out of my Spirit on all mankind, and your sons and daughters will prophesy. Your old men will dream dreams, your young men will see visions. Even on the male and female servants I will pour out My Spirit in those days. I will display wonders in the sky and on the earth, blood, fire, and columns of smoke. The sun will be turned into darkness, and the moon into blood. Before the great and awesome day of the Lord comes. And it will come about that whoever calls on the name of the Lord shall be saved."**
> Joel 2:28-32.

It is no surprise then that the Church has always been a watchman on the tower, looking out for the culmination of our day and the emergence of a new day; but would the Church be able to *recognize* the end of days when it comes?

The disciples had similar concerns and posed three penetrating questions to Jesus as they sat with him on the Mount of Olives. Here are the questions that they asked:

> **When shall these things be?**
>
> **What shall be the sign of thy coming?**
>
> **What shall be the sign of the end of the world?**

Generation after generation has searched valiantly with both eyes open for the end of time. The world, however, continued to revolve around the sun, despite any global pandemic or otherwise smaller outbreak of infirmity, war or natural disaster that threatened to minimize the human population on earth.

Yet Jesus had been specific in his response to the questions posed by the disciples. He understood clearly what they were asking and accordingly gave a clear response in **Matthew 24:4-51**,

> *"And Jesus answered and said unto them, 'Take heed that no man deceives you. For many shall come in my name, saying, I am Christ; and shall deceive many. And you shall hear of wars and rumors of wars; see that ye be not troubled; for all these*

things must come to pass, but the end is not yet. For nation shall rise against nation, and kingdom against kingdom: and there shall be famines, and pestilences, and earthquakes, in divers places. All these are the beginning of sorrows". (vs 4-8)

Our Lord was not finished; more details poured out,

"Then shall they deliver you up to be afflicted and shall kill you: and ye shall be hated of all nations for my name's sake. And then shall many be offended, and shall betray one another, and shall hate one another. And many false prophets shall rise and shall deceive many. And because iniquity shall abound, the love of many shall wax cold. But he that shall endure unto the end, the same shall be saved. And this gospel of the kingdom shall be preached in all the world for a witness unto all nations; and then shall the end come", (vs 9-14).

This had been a fascinating treatise and the disciples were spellbound! Were all these signs and manifestations really going to happen? They had never heard such a dramatic ending of the world they lived in!

Jesus could sense their confusion and hunger to know more so He added to the story that would end civilization on earth as we know it.

> *When ye shall therefore see the abomination of desolation, spoken of by Daniel the prophet, stand up in the holy place, then let them which be in Judea flee into the mountains.*
>
> *Let him which is on the housetop not come down to take anything out of his house: Neither let him which is in the field return back to take his clothes.*
>
> *And woe unto them that are with child, and to them that give suck in those days! But pray ye that your flight be not in the winter, neither on the sabbath day: For then shall be great tribulation, such as was not since the beginning of the world to this time, no, nor ever shall be"* (vs 15-21).

Then, Jesus became more specific concerning the types of people that would command this evil at the end of time,

> *And except those days should be shortened, there should no flesh be saved: but for the elect's sake those days shall be shortened. Then if any man shall say unto you, Lo, here is*

Christ, or there; believe it not. For there shall arise false christs, and false prophets, and shall show great signs and wonders; insomuch that if it were possible, they shall deceive the very elect.

Behold, I have told you before. Wherefore if they shall say unto you, Behold, he is in the desert; go not forth; behold, he is in the secret chambers; believe it not. For as the lightning cometh out of the east, and shineth even unto the west; so, shall also the coming of the Son of man be. For wheresoever the carcass is, there will be eagles gathered there.

Immediately after the tribulation of those days shall the sun be darkened, and the moon shall not give her light, and the stars shall fall from heaven, and the powers of the heavens shall be shaken.

And then shall appear the sign of the Son of man in heaven: and then shall all the tribes of the earth mourn, and they shall see the Son of man coming in the clouds of heaven with power and great glory. And he shall send his angels with a great sound of a trumpet, and they shall gather together his elect from the four winds, from one end of heaven to the other.

Now learn a parable of the fig tree; when his branch is yet tender, and putteth forth leaves, ye know that summer is nigh: so likewise ye, when ye shall see all these things, know that it is near, even at the doors. Verily I say unto you, this generation shall not pass, till all these things be fulfilled.

Heaven and earth shall pass away, but my words shall not pass away. But of that day and hour knoweth no man, no not the angels of heaven, but my Father only. But as the days of Noe were, so shall also the coming of the Son of man be. For as in the days that were before the flood they were eating and drinking, marrying and giving in marriage, and until the day that Noe entered into the ark, And knew not until the flood came, and took them all away; so shall also the coming of the Son of man be", (vs 22-39).

Then came chilling visuals,

"Then shall two be in the field; the one shall be taken, and the other left. Two women shall be grinding at the mill; and the one shall be taken, and

the other left. Watch therefore: for ye know not what hour your Lord doth come.

Do you not know this, that if the good man of the house had know in what watch the thief would come, he would have watched, and would not have suffered his house to be broken up. Therefore, be ye also ready: for in such an hour as ye think not the Son of man cometh, (vs 40-44).

Will we be ready?

"Who then is a faithful and wise servant, whom his lord hath made ruler over his household, to give them meat in due season? Blessed is that servant, whom his lord when he cometh shall find so doing. Verily I say unto you, that he shall make him ruler over all his goods. But and if that evil servant shall say in his heart, My lord delayeth his coming; And shall begin to smite his fellow servants, and to eat and drink with the drunken. The lord of that servant shall come in a day when he looketh not for him, and in an hour that he is not aware of, And, shall cut him asunder, and appoint him his portion with the hypocrites: there shall be

weeping and gnashing of teeth", (vs 45-51).

Weeping and gnashing of teeth?

For all of eternity?

Scholars have dedicated many hours of their lives to dissect and pull apart the prophetic books of the Bible in the search for clear-cut clues that would hint at the beginning of the "end of time."

We have only heard about some of the events that have played out on planet earth; events that were disclosed prior by the prophets of God under the inspiration of the Holy Spirit, who outlined in vivid and detailed form the things that were soon to come.

Doom! Calamities! Natural Disasters! Global Pandemics! Worldwide Pandemonium! All setting the stage for the rise and emergence of a New World Order and later on, the dawning of a new day.

CHAPTER 1

CHAOS!
(The future)

"But when ye shall see the abomination of desolation, spoken of by Daniel the prophet, standing where it ought not, (let him that readeth understand), then let them that be in Judaea flee to the mountains", Mark 13:14.

To pursue the last days biblically, we need a second source of information from a major figure in scripture to whom God revealed these truths.

Daniel is one of the prophets God has used to give detailed glimpses into the future. All the prophets have faithfully recorded the events to come and presented these sightings to us through the Bible.

We are beginning to see the unfolding of these events in our modern era. It is just as described, but experiencing it gives it more vivacity, thus making it more than a mental assent to a lecture in prophecy. The reality is that the unfolding is happening right before our very eyes.

A few months prior to the writing of this book, the human perception is that we were too wealthy, too resourceful, too scientifically advanced, too technologically savvy, too innovative, too modern, too sophisticated to envisage the faintest idea that a flu-like virus could bring the world to its knees.

We were wrong!

Daniel was requoted in the New Testament,

> **"While they are saying, *"Peace and safety!"* then destruction will come upon them suddenly like labour pains upon a woman with child, and they will not escape"**, 1 Thessalonians 5:3

In early 2020, the earth began experiencing a global epidemic of immeasurable proportions as a contagious disease moved its way across the globe, taking the lives of the weakest and oldest among us, and mentally assaulting the strongest.

There is pandemic and worldwide fear as governments immediately mobilize themselves, propelled into action to prevent the localized spread of this deadly virus. Every human being is affected in some way: some made moderately, critically and even fatally ill, while others are affected mentally, emotionally and financially.

This microscopic element, the Novel Coronavirus, Covid-19 for short, caused the deaths of hundreds of thousands of people in Italy, China, Spain, Great Britain, Australia, Russia, and the United States.

This, unknown disease, exposed humanity to the grim reality that we are not who we thought we were, and that we were not as prepared as we thought we were. We are vulnerable. We are exposed. We are finite. We are fallible. We are human.

"The end of days is **<u>here</u>**!" is the initial cry of both the religious and non- religious communities. The Covid-19 pandemic served not only as proof of the fulfillment of cataclysmic events spoken of in the book of Revelation, but also a reality check that when it did occur that the world was ill-prepared to cope with it. It revealed that the vast wealth and cutting-edge technologies of the world would not be able to withstand the things that would be unleashed upon this world leading up to, and during the tribulation.

Covid19 was a window into a future that should have been avoided at all cost, yet earth soon found itself in the clutches of its merciless grip! It begs to question, "If this is not the worst, then how are we going to handle it when the worst comes?"

> *If thou hast run with the footmen, and they have wearied thee, then how canst thou contend with horses? and if in the land of peace, wherein thou trustest, they wearied thee, then how wilt thou do in the swelling of Jordan?* Jeremiah 12:5

Make no mistake about it, worse is coming. What we are experiencing now represents the hoof-beats of the impending Horsemen of the Apocalypse as detailed by the Apostle John in Revelation. What then is it going to be like when these Horsemen ride into our existence? Whether we were ready or not, they will make their deadly presence known, and it will be everybody's reality, with no exemptions.

In the past, technology has allowed us to view different pandemics from the safety of our own homes. There have been other outbreaks of disease and calamities, some of which were brought under control quickly through vaccines and other scientific interventions. We observed the emergence and onslaught of the Ebola virus, the Severe Acute Respiratory Syndrome (SARS), swine and bird flu and other influenzas affecting different parts of the world; but for the most part, we were privy to watch their unfolding from a safe distance. We knew that in order to avoid some things, we simply needed to avoid travelling to the affecting areas. If we did travel, there were usually contingencies in place to protect or treat the infected.

Yet this outbreak is different. There seems to be no answers and experts seem helpless. It is as if a declaration is being made that when real calamities begin, man would be helpless to curtail it, despite our seeming technological and medical advancement.

Other influenzas have taken more lives than Covid-19, yet there is this global anxiety over this seemingly new epidemic as if there had been nothing else like it before. In fact, we have never seen anything like this before… Humanity had suffered from viruses and diseases attacking the human body in the past, but we had vaccines and cures to deal with them. As I am writing this book, the numbers of confirmed cases of and deaths from coronavirus keep climbing. We will have to wait and see what the outcome of this killer virus will be. It is too early to tell. One thing we know for sure is that Covid-19 has served as a wake-up call on a global scale as the effects of it are universally felt. We see clearly now how a contagious virus can impact the entire human population. Revelation spoke about some of the fallout that would result from a disease like this one. It may not be the actual devastation described in the Bible, but this is giving us a foretaste of what is to come.

This single event has disturbed the established economic order that we are accustomed to. Financial transactions are being done electronically at a rate never expected to be seen. Every stock market in the world has crashed, ushering in a world-wide recession. Calls are now being made with a much louder pitch for a coming together of nations into a single world community to better deal with these issues.

Is this Covid-19 event a mere chance occurrence or is it precipitating other events, like world-wide vaccine, restriction of movements, a type of police state that can dictate when one can leave home and you have to remain inside. Is the pandemic a 'pandemic'? Food for thought…

Towards one world, one government
By Tim Hewitt-Coleman - 15 April 2020

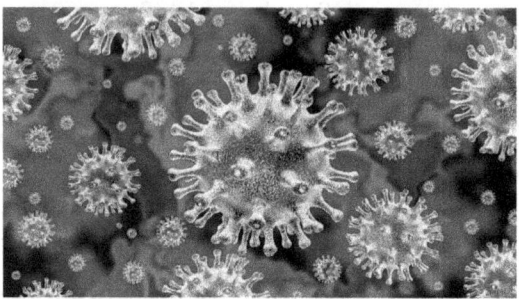

Image: 123RF/lightwise

There can be no doubt the Covid-19 crisis is making it abundantly obvious that the world's political systems are not designed (if they are designed at all) to address any of the significant threats that face our species.

As we speak, governments, presidents and sovereigns around the world are attempting to combat a global pandemic with political mechanisms and tools evolved to deal with challenges and threats at state level.

This will simply not do!

Climate change is a global problem; nuclear proliferation is a global problem; human trafficking is a global problem; as are poverty, overpopulation, migration, water scarcity and habitat destruction of both wild animals and people.

The threats we face as a species today require that we take immediate action to move to the next logical step in political organisation.

This is the incredibly complicated step of forming a new and overarching global government.

This is where our energy should be focused, debating and discussing what this kind of government should look like and what its powers should be.

The discussion must start now, ahead of the next crisis that we know will come and whose shape we know we are notoriously bad at predicting.

We need to know that the conspiracy theorists, the flat-earthers and the anti-vaxxer types will have a lot to say about a "return to colonialism" and the illuminati lizard people taking over.

We will need to rationally and calmly weather this storm.

Each of us will need to take to the streets (or to Twitter) and make our voices heard in what will surely be a brutal fight towards One World, with One Government.

We may, with time, come to see this pinnacle of all achievements as the lasting legacy of this terrible virus.

The Guardian

Gordon Brown calls for global government to tackle coronavirus

Ex-PM at centre of 2008 banks rescue suggests taskforce of leaders and health experts

Larry Elliott *Economics editor*   Thu 26 Mar 2020

Gordon Brown has urged world leaders to create a temporary form of global government to tackle the twin medical and economic crises caused by the Covid-19 pandemic.

A virtual meeting of the G20 group of developed and developing countries, chaired by Saudi Arabia, will be held on Thursday, but Brown said it would have been preferable to have also included the UN security council.

"This is not something that can be dealt with in one country," he said. "There has to be a coordinated global response."

"This is first and foremost a medical emergency and there has to be joint action to deal with that. But the more you intervene to deal with the medical emergency, the more you put economies at risk."

Brown said there had been resistance in 2008 to using the G20 as a vehicle for tackling the financial crisis, but that it should be clear to world leaders that there was no possibility of a go-it-alone approach working.

Stay tuned…

As this event is ravaging the world, there is another kind of epidemic that is unleashing damage of a different sort—nation against nation, to the death.... The word translated nations here is "ethos". Ethos against ethos. It is from this word we get ethnic. It is speaking about ethnic or racial groups hitting out against each other, in a very intense and volatile way. We are seeing this manifested before our eyes in a pronounced way, never before seen. The death of a black man in the United States city of Minnesota has caused an ethnic revolt never before seen.

This constant jockeying among countries, the constant accusations, espionage, and mistrust amongst leaders has set us in a perfect place for global war! This conflict between nations becomes more perilous by the day. North Korea versus the U.S. and their South Korean counterparts; America vs Iran; The U.S. in a battle of words and policies with Russia; Saudi Arabia versus Iran; Nations in a death struggle within Africa, and dozens of other conflicts flaring up around the world.

The scariest battle is the United States versus Red China. This seems to be on the horizon as the United States of America tries to maintain the status as the only superpower since the collapse of the Union of Soviet Socialist Republics (USSR), and China is pushing to demonstrate its ascendency and justify its right to superpower status.

The Bible is not surprised at this hatred among countries,

> *"For nation shall rise against nation, and kingdom against kingdom: and there shall be earthquakes in divers places, and there shall be famines and troubles: these are the beginnings of sorrows"* St. Mark 13:8.

The Word of God becomes more ominous in its prophecy here,

> *"You will be hearing of wars and rumours of wars. See that you are not frightened, for those things must take place, but that is not the end".* St. Matthew 24:6

That is not the end. Have mercy on us, Lord!

Added to this upheaval, is an increase famine. Famine is now being experienced in parts of Africa due to locust infestation and the worsening effects of restrictions imposed in light of the Covid-19 pandemic.

Many have challenged past prophetic interpretations that famine will be a sign of the end times. They make the challenge on the basis that in the 21st century, technology and food production methods allow for surplus and more infection resistant yields and thus the eradication of starvation. It makes good argument, but in reality, it is not so. Let us look at some extracts of the glaring stories and headlines in some international news media:

The Guardian

'Millions hang by a thread': extreme global hunger compounded by Covid-19 Coronavirus 'potentially catastrophic' for nations already suffering food insecurity caused by famine, migration and unemployment

Peter Beaumont Tue 21 Apr 2020 16.01 BST

The warning from the World Food Programme (WFP) that 265 million people could be pushed into acute food insecurity by Covid-19, almost doubling last year's total, is based on a complex combination of factors.

WFP's latest warning underlines the increasing concern among experts in the field that for many the biggest impact will not be the disease, but the hunger hanging off its coat tails.

While the majority of people suffering acute food insecurity in 2019 lived in countries affected by conflict (77 million), climate change (34 million) and economic crises (24 million people), the coronavirus has massively complicated existing crises and threatens to worsen others.

"Rising unemployment and under-employment and decreasing purchasing power will have serious consequences for poor and vulnerable populations in countries already dealing with crises such as conflict and/or ongoing economic and political turmoil," the report said.

As WFP's chief economist Arif Husain warned, "Covid-19 is potentially catastrophic for millions who are already hanging by a thread. It is a hammer blow for millions more who can only eat if they earn a wage. Lockdowns and global economic recession have already decimated their nest eggs. It only takes one more shock – like Covid-19 – to push them over the edge. We must collectively act now to mitigate the impact of this global catastrophe."

The new warning reinforces concern sounded by Lola Castro, regional director of WFP for southern Africa, last month. She said the interruption of food programmes for millions of people in the 12 countries that they cover, which have experienced three years of poor harvests because of drought, would have a "critical impact".

Hungry in a world of plenty: millions on the brink of famine--- Oxfam International

Today, the world stands on the brink of unprecedented famines. About 30 million people are experiencing alarming hunger, severe levels of food insecurity and malnutrition in north-eastern Nigeria, South Sudan, Somalia, and Yemen. 10 million of them are facing emergency and famine conditions. Famine is already likely happening in parts of northern Nigeria, while Yemen and Somalia are on the brink. Thanks to aid efforts, it has been pushed back in South Sudan but the food crisis continues to spread across the country.

The New York Times

Instead of Coronavirus, the Hunger Will Kill Us.' A Global Food Crisis Looms.
The world has never faced a hunger emergency like this, experts say. It could double the number of people facing acute hunger to 265 million by the end of this year.

By **Abdi Latif Dahir** April 22, 2020

NAIROBI, Kenya — In the largest slum in Kenya's capital, people desperate to eat set off a stampede during a recent giveaway of flour and cooking oil, leaving scores injured and two people dead.
In India, thousands of workers are lining up twice a day for bread and fried vegetables to keep hunger at bay.

And across Colombia, poor households are hanging red clothing and flags from their windows and balconies as a sign that they are hungry.

"We don't have any money, and now we need to survive," said Pauline Karushi, who lost her job at a jewelry business in Nairobi, and lives in two rooms with her child and four other relatives. "That means not eating much."

The coronavirus pandemic has brought hunger to millions of people around the world. National lockdowns and social distancing measures are drying up work and incomes, and are likely to disrupt agricultural production and supply routes — leaving millions to worry how they will get enough to eat. The coronavirus has sometimes been called an equalizer because it has sickened both rich and poor, but when it comes to food, the commonality ends. It is poor people, including large segments of poorer nations, who are now going hungry and facing the prospect of starving.

"The coronavirus has been anything but a great equalizer," said Asha Jaffar, a volunteer who brought food to families in the Nairobi slum of Kibera after the fatal stampede. "It's been the great revealer, pulling the curtain back on the class divide and exposing how deeply unequal this country is."

Already, 135 million people had been facing acute food shortages, but now with the pandemic, 130 million more could go hungry in 2020, said Arif Husain, chief economist at the World Food Program, a United Nations agency. Altogether, an estimated 265 million people could be pushed to the brink of starvation by year's end.

"We've never seen anything like this before," Mr. Husain said. "It wasn't a pretty picture to begin with, but this makes it truly unprecedented and uncharted territory."

The world has experienced severe hunger crises before, but those were regional and caused by one factor or another — extreme weather, economic downturns, wars or political instability.

"Instead of coronavirus, the hunger will kill us," said Mr. Singh, who was hoping to eat his first meal in a day. Migrants waiting in food lines have fought each other over a plate of rice and lentils. Mr. Singh said he was ashamed to beg for food but had no other option.

"The lockdown has trampled on our dignity," he said. The effects of the restrictions "may cause more suffering than the disease itself," said Kurt Tjossem, regional vice president for East Africa at the International Rescue Committee.

The pandemic is also slowing efforts to deal with the historic locust plague that has been ravaging the East and Horn of Africa. The outbreak is the worst the region has seen in decades and comes on the heels of a year marked by extreme droughts and floods. But the arrival of billions of new swarms could further

> deepen food insecurity, said Cyril Ferrand, head of the Food and Agriculture Organization's resilience team in eastern Africa.
>
> Travel bans and airport closures, Mr. Ferrand said, are interrupting the supply of pesticides that could help limit the locust population and save pastureland and crops.

On the technology side, we see the proposed widespread of 5G Technology. Privacy concerns are at the top of the list regarding its wholesale implementation as the world becomes physically distant but socially close at the touch of a button. Linked to 5G is the enhanced identification and surveillance system. (This matter will be discussed further in Chapter 3).

No need to say anymore. The Bible is never wrong. We need to take heed.

The entire world is suffering to some degree or another; the economy is failing, the full effect it not yet felt because all the focus and resources are expended on containment and preventing further spread of the coronavirus. All these things are converging (happening at the same time) and this is the first time in history that we are seeing this kind of convergence.

Based on what we see unfolding, the stage is being set for a massive shift from how things were. The parallels between what is happening in our world now and what the Bible has prophesied are striking.

We can argue that every generation has seen war and heard of rumors of wars. Yet, we cannot take away the fact that Jesus gave these specific things to look for as the very signs that will signal the approach of the end.

I believe that the rapid emergence of all these signs, along with the fact that they are all converging at this point in time in history is significant.

When we as Christians highlight that we were in a special time in history because of the rapidly unfolding events taking place, of which Jesus spoke about in St. Matthew, many thought that we were just being alarmist and merely trying to scare people to God. Many said we had no argument grounded in scientific facts, and our heralding is scoffed at by some members in academia, in the higher classes of society—in fact in all levels of society, as there are several who do not believe and dismiss our warnings about the end times.

What are the things that as Christians we are constantly echoing?

Society will degenerate and get progressively worse. People will become more barbaric and callous in their dealings with each other.

There is a plot and a well-organized programme to break down the sovereignty of nations and bring the world together under one governmental system. This plot will be headed by an evil individual infused with satanic powers and who will ultimately rule the world by the hand of the devil himself. Those of us in church circles describe this person who will lead this government as none other than the Antichrist.

There is also a well-organized plan to change the entire economic and monetary order so that there would be full control of economies to allow for the uniting of nations into a global economy. To allow for this, cash would be disbanded as the basis of exchange and transactions would be done electronically. This would enable every transaction to be evilly monitored in order that full economic control can be maintained.

To do the electronic transactions, there would be the need for swipe cards. This insidious process would eventually be replaced by an electronic system that would operate from the right hand and forehead. All transactions will require electronic exchange and through this process the mark of the Antichrist would be unleashed on the peoples of the world. In church circles we call this system the Mark of the Beast - 666. Without personally receiving this electronic transaction system (in the right hand or on the forehead) one will not be able to buy or sell.

There is no doubt that there is a calendar that is being adhered to in relation to these end time matters, thus the speed with which we are seeing the orchestration of global events.

The massive roll out of the 5G telecommunication network...

The global health crisis...

The proposed institution of identification and surveillance systems...

The haste in trying to establish the One World Order Economy...

The push for acceptance of a One World Government...

Then famine in Africa again!...

PAUSE!...

All of this together is definitely tumultuous, definitely chaotic. Something is definitely amiss, and we need to be awakened. All these events, occurrences, inventions, etc. are happening with dizzying speed. Life on a roller-coaster...the highs, the lows, the sharp bends and sudden plunges Change is the only constant. The puzzle-pieces are being fitted; the image shall soon be revealed. Nothing happens by chance. All is orchestrated. Out of this chaos will emerge a system of cruelty and death, but the bitter medicine is given in doses, making its use more acceptable to the masses, having an 'altruistic' aim, but in the end making mankind no more than automatic slaves.

Conspiracy Theories? Hardly. This is Bible! The hoof-beats are coming. Beware…

CHAPTER 2

THE HORSEMEN ARE COMING!

There are four horsemen recorded in Revelation 6. These four riders appeared to the Apostle John in a vision while he was banished on the isle of Patmos for the testimony of the Lord Jesus. What is the significance of these horsemen? What do they really represent? The mere mention of the term *'the horsemen of the apocalypse'* inspires caution, fear, and dread in the hearts of men.

The last book in the Bible, is in fact, the revelation of Jesus Christ and not the revelation of St. John. The Apostle John was merely the scribe, writing what Jesus had revealed to him.

Revelation Chapter 1: 10-13 states,

> *"I was in the spirit on the Lord's day and heard behind me a great voice, as of a trumpet saying, "I am Alpha and Omega, the first and the last:, and what thou seest, write in a book and send it unto the seven churches which are in Asia; unto Ephesus, and unto Smyrna and unto Pergamos and unto Thyatira, and unto Sardis, and unto Philadelphia, and unto Laodicea". And I turned to see the voice that spoke with me. And being turned, I*

> *saw seven golden candlesticks; and in the midst of the seven candle sticks one like unto the Son of man, clothed with a garment down to the foot..."*

Finally, verse 19 says, **"Write the things which thou hast seen, and the things which are, and the things shall be hereafter".**

It is important to make the point here, that Revelation is not a book of secrets or hidden messages that are dark and not meant to be understood. On the contrary, 'revelation' comes from the Greek word 'apokalypsis' from which we get the English term apocalypse', which means "unveiling or uncovering". Hence the book is called the Apocalypse.

Revelation Chapters 6 – 19 reveals 21 judgements that will be unleashed on this world. A lot of things are coming that will be horrific in nature, and cataclysmic in proportion. These 21 judgements are broken out into 3 distinct series of future judgements. First, there is the **seven-seal judgements**, secondly there is the **seven trumpet judgements** and thirdly, there is the **seven vials judgements**. Each of these are unique events that will take place in the tribulation period. This tribulation period is also referred to as '*The time of Jacob's trouble*' and represents a time where the wrath of God is going to be poured out upon mankind.

The first of the set of judgements is from the seven-sealed judgement as recorded in Revelation Chapter 6: 1-8,

> *"And I saw when the lamb opened one of the seals, and I heard, as it were a noise of thunder, one of the four beasts saying, Come and see. And I saw and behold a white horse: and he that sat on him had a now; and a crown was given unto him: and he went forth conquering, and to conquer. And when he had opened the second seal, I heard the second beast say, Come and see.*
>
> *And there went out another horse that was red: and power was given to him that sat thereon to take peace from the earth, and that they should kill one another: and there was given unto him a great sword. And when he had opened the third seal, I heard the beast say, Come and see. And I beheld, and lo a black horse: and he that sat on him had a pair of balances in his hand. And I heard a voice in the midst of the four beasts say. A measure of wheat for a penny, and three measures of barley for a penny; and see thou hurt not the oil and the wine. And when he had opened the fourth seal, I heard the voice of the fourth beast say, Come see.*

> *And I looked and behold a pale horse: and his name that sat on him was Death, and Hell followed with him.*
>
> *And power was given unto them over the fourth part of the earth, to kill with sword and with hunger, and with death and with the beasts of the earth'. And so, this introduces the four horsemen riding unto the scene".*

With this understanding that God is revealing or making known things that must come to pass, let us now turn our attention to the first horseman of the Apocalypse.

The First Horseman

> *"And I saw and behold a white horse: and he that sat on him had a bow; and a crown was given unto him: and he went forth conquering, and to conquer,"* (Revelation 6:2)

As it now stands, the world is in a state of war even though no shots are as yet being fired. Look at what is happening in North Korea. They are constantly testing long-range missiles. On June 13, 2020 North Korea threatened to attack South Korea, in languages that the world community took very seriously.

North Korea blows up inter-Korean liaison office near border with South

Kang Jin-kyu. AFP June 16, 2020, 1:47 PM EDT

Smoke rise from North Korea's Kaesong industrial complex where a Korean liaison office was blown up by Pyongyang

Smoke rise from North Korea's Kaesong industrial complex where a Korean liaison office was blown up by Pyongyang (AFP Photo/STR).

North Korea blew up an inter-Korean liaison office on its side of the border on Tuesday, triggering broad international condemnation after days of virulent rhetoric from Pyongyang.

The demolition came after Kim Yo Jong -- the powerful sister of North Korean leader Kim Jong Un -- said at the weekend the "useless north-south joint liaison office" would soon be seen "completely collapsed".

Footage of the explosion released by Seoul's presidential Blue House showed a blast rolling across several buildings just across the border in Kaesong, with a nearby tower partially collapsing as clouds of smoke rose into the sky.

Analysts say Pyongyang may be seeking to manufacture a crisis to increase pressure on Seoul while nuclear negotiations with Washington are at a standstill.

After an emergency meeting, the National Security Council said it would "react strongly" if Pyongyang "continues to take steps that aggravate the situation".

"All responsibility for repercussions stemming from this action falls squarely on the North," it added.

The US, European Union and Russia all called for restraint.

Consider the rise of China and the fear among their neighbours in the region as a result. Why is this so? China is flexing its economic and military muscles to take over the entire South China Sea area to the exclusion of all its neighbours.

The situation in the Middle East is a melting pot of imminent danger. Iran and Iraq have sworn to erase Israel off the map. Iran, Syria, and Israel are playing cat and mouse with each other with real bombs.

Hezbollah, originally in Lebanon, is now extending into Syria and are boasting of missiles with the ability to reach into the heartlands of Israel and they vow to use them.

Just when the world thought that the Islamic State of Iraq and Syria (ISIS) was defeated and terrorism was becoming a thing of the past, the Taliban in Afghanistan is on the rise again.

Russia just months ago had two of their bombers intercepted over the North Sea in the United Kingdom (UK) as they approached the UK's air space.

This is just the tip of the iceberg that shows the state of distress and constant tension evident in the world. It is within this context that leaders around the world are crying out for someone of sufficient stature to step-up-to-the-plate and provide strong, solid leadership to resolve these issues that threaten not only the stability of the world, but its very existence.

Long before world conditions reached to this point of chaos and near anarchy, there were cries for such a maximum leader to come on the scene. Listen to the words of Paul-Henri Spaak (1899 - 1972), former Belgian Prime Minister, one of the principal architects of what is now the European Union (EU), and former Secretary General of NATO (North

Atlantic Treaty Organization) (1957-1960): "**What we want is a man of sufficient stature to hold the alliances of all people and to lift us out of the economic morass into which we are sinking. Send us such a man, and be he god or the devil, we will receive him**" (Christians Together, 2012)

This is exactly how the Bible indicated that the Antichrist would make his entry on the world stage! I am not presenting fiction brothers and sisters, this is reality. Prepare therefore for the rider of the first horse of the apocalypse, the rider on the white horse.

Now, there is a lot of misunderstanding as to the true identity of this first horseman. Some have suggested that this rider represents Christians taking charge of earthly governments and conquering in the name of the Lord Jesus Christ. Some suggest that it is a representation of Christ's Second Coming, and some even believe it represents the preaching of the gospel of Christ all over the world which will result in the conversion of man for Almighty God. The truth?: The rider on the white horse of Revelation 6 is none other than a counterfeit Christ.

Let's compare Revelation 6:2 with Revelation 19:11-15. This will clarify that the rider of Revelation 6:2 is a counterfeit who will fool many.

Notice that the Christ of Revelation 19, Who also rides on a white horse, has a sword protruding out of

His mouth and not a bow in His hand as Revelation 6.

The Word of God is symbolically represented as a two-edged sword according to Hebrews 4:12 which states, *"for the word of God is quick, and powerful, and sharper than any two-edged sword, piercing even to the dividing asunder of soul and spirit, and of the joints and marrow, and is a discerner of the thoughts and intents of the heart"*.

> Revelation 19:11-15
> *And I saw heaven opened, and behold a white horse; and he that sat upon him was called Faithful and True, and in righteousness he doth judge and make war.*
> *His eyes were as a flame of fire, and on his head were many crowns; and he had a name written, that no man knew, but he himself.*
> *And he was clothed with a vesture dipped in blood: and his name is called The Word of God.*
> *And the armies which were in heaven followed him upon white horses, clothed in fine linen, white and clean.*
> *And out of his mouth goeth a sharp sword, that with it he should smite the nations: and he shall rule them with a rod of iron: and he treadeth the winepress of the fierceness and wrath of Almighty God.*

Jesus Christ is coming to judge the nations with His words, <u>hence the rider with the sword in His mouth</u> is none other than the Lord Jesus Christ.

It is also important to note that there are two different time periods between Revelation 6 and Revelation 19, proving that they could not be the same person, the same Christ.

The white horse of Revelation 6 is introduced when the first seal is opened. It is the first of a series of dramatic events depicting the end times and is at the beginning of the Tribulation Period. It's close association with the three other horsemen helps to highlight this fact.

The Second Coming of Christ, or His revelation according to Revelation 19, on the other hand, ushers in the end of these dramatic end time events. These take place at the end of the tribulation period just before the establishment of the millennial reign of Jesus Christ. Therefore, these two riders are separated by years, thus both scriptures are referring to two different persons at two different times. The big question then is, "Who is the rider of Revelation 6:2?"As just stated he is the Antichrist and it is important for us to note that the Antichrist does not only mean "one who is opposed to Chris" but it also means "INSTEAD of Christ!!" Therefore, he is presenting himself as the Christ, (instead of the Christ), and his intention is to rule the world.

The adversary knows that it is prophesied that Jesus Christ will sit on the throne of His father David and He will rule over all Israel, and from Jerusalem, over the entire earth! (St. Luke 1:32-33). Satan himself knows this and so just like any counterfeit, he is pushing to establish himself as "Christ", different from the legitimate Christ which is to come.

This Antichrist is going to sit in the temple at Jerusalem where Christ is supposed to be sitting upon his return to earth, and he is going to present himself as king and the ruler over Israel and the entire world. He is a wolf in sheep's clothing, plotting to ravage the world. A counterfeit Christ he is indeed.

He is also described in scriptures as the 'Man of sin", "The son of perdition", and "the Wicked one". He is also called "the Beast" and this is not how he physically looks, but is related to his character, which is described in Revelation 13:2-6,

> *"And the beast which I saw was like a leopard, and his feet were like those of a bear, and his mouth like the mouth of a lion. And the dragon gave him his power and his throne and great authority. I saw one of his heads as if it had been slain, and his fatal wound was healed. And the whole earth was amazed and followed after the beast; they worshipped the dragon because he gave his authority to the beast; and they*

worshipped the beast, saying. "Who is like the beast, and who is able to wage war with him?" There was given to him a mouth speaking arrogant words and blasphemies, and authority to act for forty-two months was given him. And he opened his mouth in blasphemies against God, to blaspheme His name and His tabernacle, that is, those who dwell in heaven."

He will be a monster of immense proportion in character and arrogance. Yet men will not know that he has this dark side because he is coming with fair speech.

Every step of the way the Antichrist will try to counterfeit the true God of heaven. The legitimate Christ of Revelation 19 is in fact the King of Kings and Lord of Lords. True to form, the Antichrist will proclaim himself to be God,

"Let no one in any way deceive you, for it will not come unless the apostasy comes first, and the man of lawlessness is revealed, the son of destruction, who opposes and exalts himself above every so-called god or object of worship, so that he takes his seat in the temple of God, displaying himself as being God.", 2 Thessalonians 2:3.

The Antichrist comes to power through some negotiated peace arrangement and it somehow catapults him into prominence. He goes on to facilitate economic and political stability and is received nearly by all. Note the following two scriptures which highlight this:

> *"And he shall confirm the covenant with many for one week: and in the midst of the week he shall cause a sacrifice and oblation to cease, and for the overspreading of abomination."* Daniel 9:27

> *"And it was given unto him to make war with the saints, and to overcome them: and power was given him over all kindreds, and tongues, and nations, and he was given authority to rule over every tribe and people and language and nation."* Revelation 13:7.

According to the book of Daniel, he is going to be very articulate and people will be enamored by him. He will be the master of deception. The Antichrist will bring peace to the Middle East and other parts of the world that are torn by strife and he will actually facilitate a crucial peace accord to be signed between Israel and their Arab neighbours, who are sworn enemies. This is something that Israel has longed for since 1948, when they became a nation. Over the years since their rebirth, they have been in constant conflict with their neighbours. I believe that they are tired of the constant wars and fighting and so will be happy for this peace arrangement which will be palatable to them. They will not understand however that they would have signed a covenant with death and hell. They will at the time however be satisfied with the arrangements and will apparently let down their guards.

The Beast will propose policies for economic stability to the extent that the whole world will be in awe of him. This dictator will be that person who will rule quietly at first; and seem to be a man for the people but his true colours and his identity will be revealed in time. By then, it will be too late.

It is important to note that the platform is already in place to accommodate this maximum leader. If he is to rule the world, then there must be a robust communication system that allows him to have access, power and authority over nations far and wide, even while he is in one location.

The improved telecommunication system, known as the 5G network is now a reality in our world. It is already functioning. The sheer power and capacity of 5G to facilitate the electronic monitoring of all kinds of transactions, including electronic espionage by phones, computers and televisions, simultaneously across the world in multiple languages is amazing. The platform is here, and the things predicted in Revelation are literally on our doorsteps.

Whomever that man is going to be, he has the substructure fully in place that will give him that ability to reach the entire world system. He will be able to keep tabs on all the inhabitants of the world. He will know everything about us: our bank accounts, our health status and all our personal finance and business data. Scarily, he will have complete coverage of everything we do. It will appear as if this man is like a god which is very much what he thinks of himself – as God sitting in the place of God. Pure evil.

White implies pure/ But he's not, that's sure
Rising from the pit of hell/ Revealing the antichrist,
time will tell

The Second Horseman

> ***"And there went out another horse that was red: and power was given to him that sat thereon to take peace from the earth, and they should kill one another: and there was given unto him a great sword",*** Revelation 6:4.

This rider was given power and authority to take peace from the earth. This red horseman represents *war* and terror. Some might argue that there was always war even from the time that Jesus spoke in St. Matthew concerning the end times,

> *"You will be hearing of wars and rumors of wars. See that you are not frightened, for those things must take place, but that is not yet the end. For nation will rise against nation, and kingdom against kingdom, and in various places there will be famines and earthquakes",* St. Matthew 24:6

Now the rider on the first horse, as was earlier stated, brought in a kind of peace which caused the people of the world to think "peace and safety". In fact, this is a "pseudo peace". It is really a covenant with death and hell.

> *"When they shall say peace and safety; then sudden destruction cometh upon them as travail upon a woman with child"* - 1 Thessalonians 5:3.

All the so-called 'peace' will be erased by the rider of the red horse as he comes on the scene. This rider introduces to the earth a time of war, terror, and bloodshed as we have never seen.

War does not only mean the conventional battle that we are familiar with. It involves other warfare methods that we today call 'terrorism'. Think about ISIS, Al-Queda, Taliban, Boko-Haram, and other insidious groups. These are organizations that are sworn to the destruction of Israel, America and the western civilization as we know it. To achieve their objectives these groups will reign terror upon the globe with such intensity that is unimaginable. What we are witnessing today is a pre-cursor to what is to come, when the rider of the red horse is introduced. What we are witnessing today will pale in comparison to what is coming in the tribulation period.

Airports, airplanes, restaurants, malls will become free stomping ground for death and mayhem associated with the coming of this rider. On September 11, 2001, in the United States of America, two planes with passengers and crew were turned into missiles as they were flown into the Twin Towers, killing thousands of people. This dastardly, horrific act is like a Sunday School picnic compared to the devastation that is to come when this rider gallops unto the scene.

Coupled with the above, Russia is called out in scriptures to play a role in the end time wars that will take peace from the earth. You may be surprised to know that these names are still to be found in the former Soviet Union (USSR). Tobolsk, the eastern capital of the former USSR is the ancient Tubal and, Meshech is Moscow. The historical names for Moscow begin with "Meshech", then "Moshoch," it goes through a number of other renditions, and finally Moscow. Rosh is for Russia itself.

> *"You will come from your place out of the remote parts of the <u>north</u>, you and many peoples with you, all of them riding on horses, a great assembly and a mighty army; and you will come up against My people Israel like a cloud to cover the land. It shall come about in the last days that I will bring you against My land, so that the nations may know Me when I am sanctified through you before their eyes, O Gog"* - Ezekiel 38:15-16.

In what will trigger one of the fiercest battles of all the times, Russia moves in on Israel. Note that Russia is directly north of Israel and will be involved in a major attack on her near the end of days. It is during this latter period of war that a third of the inhabitants of this world will be destroyed, Revelation 9:18 will indeed be a terrible day. Woe to the inhabitants of the earth.

> *"A third of mankind was killed by these three plagues, by the fire and the smoke and the brimstone which proceeded out their mouths."*

The woe is come clad in red! War, blood and many dead.

The Third Horseman

> *"And when he had opened the third seal, I heard the third beast say, come and see. And I beheld and lo, a black horse; and he that sat on him had a pair of balances in his hand. And I heard a voice say, A measure of wheat for a penny, and three measures of barley for a penny; and see thou hurt not the oil and the wine"* - Revelation 6:5-6.

In addition to the famine that comes as result of the wars and terrorism, there is a clear indication in the scripture of a time of serious economic hardship. The use of scales and balances convey economic and financial challenges—making ends meet and affording the necessary basics. No doubt this refers to the severe ravages of inflation of economic turmoil, and the ensuing limited purchasing power of the average person. I believe supermarket shelves will be empty in many cases, and even where there might be food on the others, the means to purchase will not be there. Hunger and general despair will prevail. An entire days' pay will yield enough for only one loaf of bread.

Yet even under these conditions as the poor get poorer and more desperate, the rich will continue to get richer, as there will be no damage to "the oil and the wine",

> *"When He broke the third seal, I heard the third living creature saying, "Come." I looked and behold, a black horse; and he who sat on it had a pair of scales in his hand. And I heard something like a voice in the centre of the four living creatures saying, "A quart of wheat for a denarius, and three quarts of barley for a denarius, and do not damage the oil and wine"* - Revelation 6: 5-6.

It is interesting to note that the black horse of famine came immediately after the red horse of war. Starvation usually ensues because of crop and livestock damages and contamination of water supplies.

As famines of 'biblical proportion' loom, Security Council urged to 'act fast'

FAO/IFAD/WFP/Michael Tewelde| In 2019, Ethiopia experienced the fifth-worst food crisis of all the countries on earth.

21 April 2020 Humanitarian Aid

The world is not only facing "a global health pandemic but also a global humanitarian catastrophe", the UN food relief agency chief told the Security Council on Tuesday via video link.

Noting that the global spread of COVID-19 (https://www.un.org/coronavirus) this year has sparked "the worst humanitarian crisis since World War Two", Executive Director of the World Food Programme (WFP (http://www1.wfp.org/)) David Beasley pointed (https://www.wfp.org/news/wfp- chief-warns-hunger-pandemic-covid-19-spreads-statement-un-security-council)to deepening crises, more frequent natural disasters and changing weather patterns, saying "we're already facing a perfect storm".

As millions of civilians in conflict-scarred nations teeter on the brink of starvation, he said, "famine is a very real and dangerous possibility".

Mr. Beasley painted a grim picture of 135 million people facing crisis levels of hunger or worse, coupled with an additional 130 million on the edge of starvation prompted by Coronavirus (https://www.un.org/coronavirus), noting that WFP currently offers a lifeline to nearly 100 million people – up from about 80 million just a few years ago.

"If we can't reach these people with the life-saving assistance they need, our analysis shows that 300,000 people could starve to death every single day over a three-month period", he upheld. "This does not include the increase of starvation due to COVID-19".

Against the backdrop that 135 million people in 55 countries experienced acute food insecurity in 2019, nearly 60 per cent of whom lived in conflict or instability, he cited Yemen as the world's worst food and malnutrition crisis this year, saying that the number of acutely food-insecure people there is "expected to exceed 17 million".

We must understand that there were famines in the past and even as you read these writings, people in different parts of the world are experiencing famine.

The Bible states that there was a famine as far back as Abraham's days (Genesis 12:10). Global famine is not new to this earth. *"...and, the famine was over all the face of the earth"*. (Genesis 41:56). See also 2 Samuel 21:1; 1 Kings 18:2; Luke 4:25; 2 Kings 6:25-29. It must be recognized, however, that the famines that are mentioned above, along with these in our times will pale in significance to what is to come! At best, even the drinking water will be measured (because of its unavailability).

A few years ago, scientists and technocrats scoffed at these predictions and tried to cast doubt on the Bible, because in their "enlightened" view these kinds of mass starvation are a thing of the past. Scientific advancement and modern farming techniques had put an end to the idea of famines ever happening again, so, they brushed aside these kinds of predictions classifying them as illogical nonsense.

The Bible is always right, and it does not matter how the "enlightened" ones try to use logics and science to reason it out. A day is coming when it will be much worse.

After war comes famine and lack
No light, no hope, just black

The Fourth Horseman

"And I looked, and behold, a <u>pale</u> horse: and his name that sat on him was Death, and Hell followed with him. And power was given unto them over the fourth part of the earth, to kill with sword, and with hunger, and with death and with the beasts of the earth."- Revelation 6:8.

Many have asked, what colour is pale? What does pale signify? A little study of this reveals the following which gives us a clue as to the significance of this pale horse. The word pale in this scripture is derived from the Greek word *"chloros"*. It is this root word that we also get "chlorophyll" (that green substance which is responsible for the green colouration in plants). The term chlorine gas is also derived from this root word. As used in this context it represents a greenish-yellow colour which so often depicts disease. Other translations use the term "a sickly pale horse". In other words, there will be a serious disease epidemic in the last days, the proportions of which has never been known. Absolutely devastating! This is probably the reason that we have death ring upon this horse, with hell following.

The Acquired Immuno-Deficiency Syndrome (AIDS), Hepatitis B and other dangerous diseases might very well be 'child's play' in comparison to what is to come. Notice the scripture also says that the beasts of the earth will be responsible for killing a large portion of mankind during that time. This could have two meanings.

Firstly, diseases/epidemics can break out as a result of animals (have you seen the news?) In 2019, the novel corona virus (covid-19) broke out in a wet market in Wuhan, China, supposedly from bats and snakes. 2009 to 2010 saw the global outbreak of swine flu (H1N1). In January 1998, reports on international news media shared that people in Hong Kong were dying because of a bird disease, passed on to humans by virtue of their consumption of chicken meat. Also, there was the 'mad cow disease' [Bovine spongiform encephalopathy (BSE)] coming out of Britain which killed individuals who consumed beef infected with a particular disease. These diseases are all animal borne. The shadow of the rider of the pale horse seems to be approaching. Beware!

Secondly, it could mean that animals will literally be attacking the human population. With war, famine and food shortage impacts the animal kingdom also. This period of time may see the beasts leaving their jungle habitat in search of food and their food could be *humankind*.

Here comes death riding on the pale

With hell behind, humanity to assail

There are great shadows overreaching our day and the objects casting these shadows are the coming horsemen. Be prepared. Awake Zion awake; awake a trim your lamps!

CHAPTER 3

THAT TERRIBLE MARK - 666

In his discourse with the disciples on the Mount of Olives, Jesus gave direct indication that a period of time was coming that was going to be extremely horrific. The events He hinted at coincided with the rule and reign of the Antichrist. Jesus outlined the conditions of that period. There will be wars, rumors of wars, nations mistrusting nations, betrayal, persecution, and death. The end times would be so devastating that if He did not literally intervene no flesh would be saved (St. Matthew 24). Why would this be the case? Because man through the prompting of Satan, was bent on destroying themselves and the planet that God has created for His sovereign purpose.

The nuclear arsenal that is presently amassed in countries around the world is enough to destroy the world many times over. Based on what Jesus said, deceit, mistrust and hatred would prevail and no doubt, mankind with these weapons in their possession will definitely attempt to use them. Our Lord, however, will save the day so there is no annihilation.

There are a few additional things about the Antichrist that I wish to point out here so that we can understand how he would transition easily as the leader of the One World Government and its economy. This period of time is fast approaching, and I will document here how close we are to being overtaken by the events that will characterize the times.

The Antichrist will be a man of significant influence; perhaps be the recipient of the Nobel peace prize and be recognized and accepted by the elite political class. This coming world leader will enter and lead us into a cashless world economy. This means that financial transactions will be done electronically where they can be fully monitored, and a system of control can be established for all citizens of the earth.

Who will pull off this technological marvel? Let the Bible tell us! Examine Revelation 13:16 -18,

> *"He causes all, both small and great, rich and poor, free and bond, to receive a mark on their right hand or on their foreheads, and that no one may buy and sell except one who has the mark or the name of the beast, or the number of his name".*

The overall system to come is laid out in this chapter of the book of Revelation. Verses 1-8 speaks of the Antichrist himself (the political leader), then verses 11-15 speak of the religious system led by the religious leader (the false prophet), and finally verses 16-18 outline the economic system and the enforcement of it.

At the writing of this book it is illegal to transact any business in cash over US$8,000 in Jamaica and even less than that in the U.S. and other places. In some jurisdictions if you are found with more than US$3,000 it is a criminal offense and has significant jail time associated with it. The point is that there is a global push to <u>eliminate</u> cash transactions and it is getting to the point where it will soon be totally outlawed! This is being introduced under the guise of preventing robberies, curtailing money laundering, etc. or as a means of convenient shopping. Either way, by coercion or cooperation, the cashless system, which will be the facilitator of the electronic One-World economy, is a reality. It is happening at this very moment.

The transition from cash to electronic/digital exchange is rapidly rising. This is not by chance at all. This is the plan being rolled out before our very eyes, all coinciding with the prophecy of Revelation 13.

At this point, only 3% of Sweden do business using cash. In the USA only 7% of transactions are by with, and in the Euro zone only 9% of the economy uses cash, and these numbers are trending down. Most of us are unaware of these facts. These countries are very close to being cashless. We are much nearer to the implementation of final things than we can ever imagine!

A one-world economy and a one-world government go hand in hand. What is at the heart of all this is control; **Satan himself seeks to have control over mankind**. This was always his strategic plan. He is fully aware of the scripture which infuriates him beyond measure!

> *"And the Lord will be King over all the earth; in that day the Lord will be the only one, and His name the only one"* - Zachariah 14:9.

As his eternal focus, the devil is seeking to be Lord over the whole earth, just as he knows Jesus will be. All the plans of man for this one- world economy, one-world government, one-world religion is inspired by Satan and the dark forces of his regime. Revelation 13:2 indicates that, ***"it is Satan which gives the Antichrist his seat, and power and authority"***.

The Antichrist has no interest in bringing convenience and fulfillment to man. He hates man and everything God created, for that matter. Anything we receive in terms of convenience is just a means to his end. Satan's entire plot is diabolical, and his ultimate agenda is for him to have control, to be in charge and rule the world, in the person of the "Son of perdition" known as the Antichrist.

Thus, that terrible mark, known as the "Mark of the Beast" represents a unique identifying system that everyone will choose to have (or be forced to have) in order to buy or sell. Without that 'Mark' no transaction can be processed. This guarantees an electronic surveillance system that can track you and your activities *en masse.*

We see clearly how the United Nations (UN) and countries with the economic might use economic sanctions to punish countries with whom they are at variance. This then becomes a weapon used to cause countries to fall in line with a particular dictate.

The question to be considered is, "Where do these dictates originate? Who is calling the shots?" This mode of operation gives a clear idea how the system will be used to enforce the will and dictates of the coming regime. Nations states will not have the economic power to oppose and will therefore conform. This kind of manipulation is taking place at this very moment and is shaping the kind of economic and social direction for countries around the world. You need to be aware that this will be part of an international system that will be used to effect worldwide control by a certain world dictator.

The prophet Daniel gives some important information about this character and his power. Let us examine two passages of scripture from the book of Daniel:

> *"And he shall speak great words against the most High, and shall wear out the saints of the most High, and think to change times and laws: and they shall be given into his hand until a time and times and the dividing of time"* - Daniel 7:25;

and, again in Daniel 8:23-25,

> *"And in the latter time of their kingdom, when the transgressors come to the full, a king of fierce countenance and understanding dark sentences shall stand up. And his power shall be mighty, but not by his own power: and he shall destroy wonderfully, and shall prosper, and practice, and shall destroy the mighty and the holy people. And through his policy also he shall cause craft to prosper in his hand, and he shall magnify himself in his heart, and by peace shall destroy many:"*

The Antichrist, as stated by Daniel, will be a person of *influence*. He will command respect and shall promote a peaceful agenda. Just like the serpent in the Garden of Eden, "the angel of light" approach has always been effective for Satan. He lulls his victims to believe in a false sense of security before he pounces! Men everywhere are crying for peace and it somehow keeps eluding them. The powerful government of the United States has made many attempts to broker peace in the Middle East, but to no avail. Human beings are totally incapable of bringing about peace. They are at the mercy of terrorist attacks and the evil leaders that incite them around the world.

People in the Middle East are reluctant to use public transport for fear that they will be the next casualty of a bombing. Those internal fears cause despair, stress, and terror. Just the way Satan likes it!

Imagine, then a dynamic leader, coming on the scene that makes certain proposals and outlines a policy that is the nearest thing to peace that the world had ever seen. Is there a chance here to unite that part of the world? Men will gladly accept this international peace pact, and on that basis, this dynamic leader comes to power. He begins with a 'harmless' offer of peace in the Middle East making people believe that it is a positive step to ending decades of war.

Remember the first horseman of the apocalypse? That rider had a bow but no arrows. Thus, he received his power not through war or a coup or any such thing, but by peaceful means. This is the trap. That is his strategy. Like a frog put into a tank of cold water, it will boil to death if the heat is slowly and cunningly heightened. The frog will lie there peaceably until it is scalded to death. That will be the method of the clever Antichrist, "Peace, brother", until it turns to death.

It is because of this approach that men and women will be totally deceived. His real character, however, is not of an altruistic Saviour, but that of a *beast*. He is named appropriately. This is because of his real character and he is evil personified.

Signs of the Antichrist

Listed below are some things that the Bible says about this Beast and what is to come:

> *"And through his shrewdness, he will cause deceit to succeed by his influence; and he will magnify himself in his heart, and he will destroy many while they are at ease. He will even oppose the Prince of princes, but he will be broken without human agency"* - Daniel 8:25

He shall come out of the people who killed Messiah the prince.

> *"Then after the sixty-two weeks the Messiah will be cut off and have nothing, and the people of prince who is to come will destroy the city and the sanctuary. And its end will come with a flood; even to the end of there will be war; desolations are determined"* - Daniel 9:26.

We know that Jesus was killed by Roman soldiers. Rome was the political hub of the European world. Thus, he is coming out of Europe. Keep your eyes focused on Europe. He will exalt himself as God.

> *"Who opposes and exalts himself above every so-called god or object of worship, so that he takes his seat in the temple of*

God, displaying himself as being God" - 2 Thessalonians 2:4.

He will blaspheme God,

> *"There was given to him a mouth speaking arrogant words and blasphemies, and authority to act for forty-two months was given to him. And he opened his mouth blasphemies against God, to blaspheme His name and His tabernacle, that is, those who dwell in heaven"* - Revelation 13:5-6.

The world will worship him,

> *"All who dwell on earth will worship him, everyone whose name has not been written from the foundation of the world in the book of life of the Lamb who has been slain"* - Revelation 13:18.

He will be charming as a he is deceitful; and as appealing as he is arrogant.

For the Antichrist to have dominion over world affairs and establish himself in a position of universal power; there must be a *system* that will facilitate his operation. That little machine called the *computer* is playing a role in establishing a system that the Antichrist will use to control and manipulate the entire world.

How will this *work?* Let me begin by using a simple local (Jamaican) example with which we can identify. We all know that sometime ago that the Jamaican Government introduced the Tax-Payer Registration Number (TRN) system. The TRN system facilitates Government's computerization programme for the Revenue Departments, and aid in improving tax administration and provide better service to the public. It is purported to help taxpayers by eliminating varied numbers and duplicated information used by the Revenue departments for the same taxpayer, and to create and maintain accurate files for taxpayers for easy retrieval. (https://www.jamaicatax-online.gov.jm/Portal/tax_faqs.html).

Without the TRN a citizen will not be able to go into the tax office to licence their motor vehicle, to sell it, or to transact some other business. He or she will be asked by the clerk; *"May I have your TRN number please"?* If that citizen does not have that number, the government representative's response will be, *"I'm sorry but we are unable to process anything for you until you get your TRN number. Please get it and come back".* Countless numbers of people in Jamaica had this experience or witnessed it happening to others in the initial phase. I hope you are beginning to see the picture.

With this TRN, an individual's personal information is placed into a computer database, the government can retrieve that information at any time. This was the simple beginning, but it gave a clear signal of how things will unfold and how there will ultimately be a record of *all* individuals with information on **everything** about them.

This system of getting detailed information about people is not limited to Jamaica or a few other countries. It is happening in *every* country in the world. It is being perpetuated everywhere as a new way of doing business. Every person will have an identification number which will allow them to transact business.

Society is moving from being paper based to being more digitally connected. Technology is rapidly advancing, and these new advancements are laying the foundation upon which the one world Order and control can be established. Let us look at some article excerpts:

On the technology side, we see the proposed widespread of 5G Technology. You may question "What is 5G Technology and how does it work?"

5G is the 5th generation mobile network. It is a new global wireless standard after 1G, 2G, 3G, and 4G networks. 5G enables a new kind of network that is designed to connect virtually everyone and everything together including machines, objects, and devices.

5G wireless technology is meant to deliver higher multi-Gbps peak data speeds, ultra low latency, more reliability, massive network capacity, increased availability, and a more uniform user experience to more users. Higher performance and improved efficiency empower new user experiences and connects new industries. (https://www.qualcomm.com/invention/5g/what-is-5g)

Initial 5G services commenced in many countries in 2019 and widespread availability of 5G is expected by 2025.

(http://www.emfexplained.info/?ID=25916)

Yet, there is more.

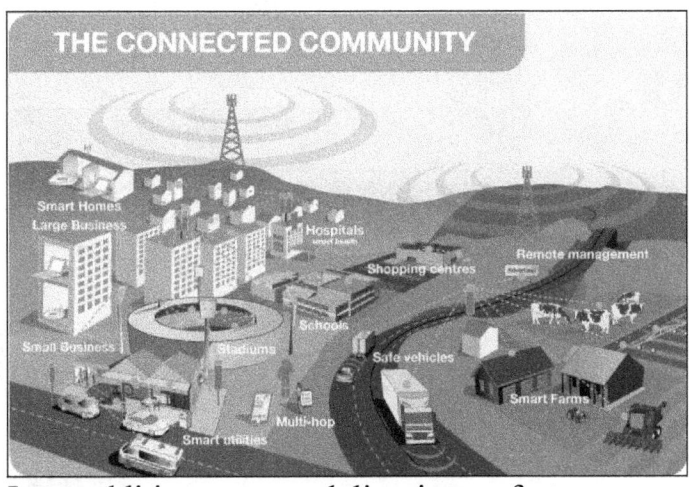

In addition to delivering faster connections and greater capacity, a very important advantage of 5G is the fast response time referred to as latency.

Latency is the time taken for devices to respond to each other over the wireless network. 3G networks had a typical response time of 100 milliseconds, 4G is around 30 milliseconds and 5G will be as low as 1 millisecond. This is virtually instantaneous opening up a new world of connected applications.

What will 5G enable?

5G will enable instantaneous connectivity to billions of devices, the Internet of Things (IoT) and a truly connected world.

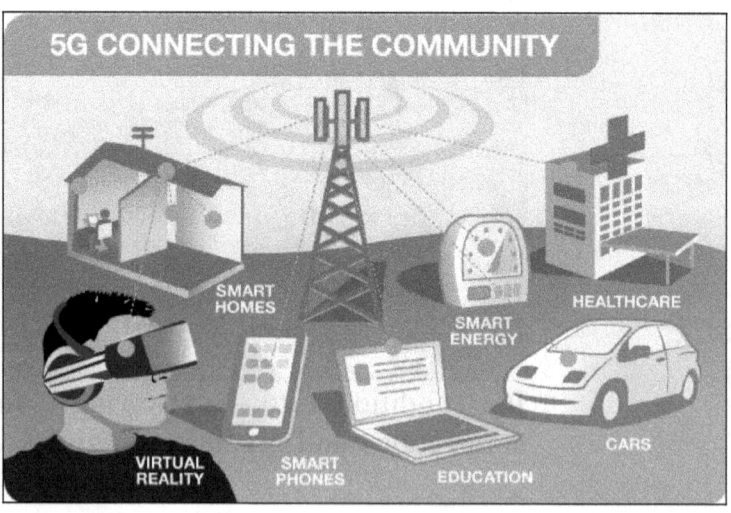

5G will provide the speed, low latency and connectivity to enable a new generation of applications, services and business opportunities that have not been seen before.

New and Emerging technologies such as virtual and augmented reality will be accessible by everyone. Virtual reality provides connected experiences that were not possible before. With 5G and VR you will be able to travel to your favourite city, watch a live football match with the feeling of being at the ground, or even be able to inspect real estate and walk through a new home all from the comfort of your couch.

5G will keep us connected in tomorrow's smart cities, smart homes and smart schools, and enable opportunities that we haven't even thought of yet. (http://www.emfexplained.info/?ID=25916)

On the surface, this improved technology comes with a lot of benefits: ease of communication, business efficiency, security, improved healthcare, agricultural efficiency, and the list can go on. It however is the base platform from which surveillance data on earth's citizenry can be gathered. This then is the heart of the matter.

In providing an update in the House of Representatives on April 28, [2020], the Most Honourable Prime Minister, Andrew Holness, shared that:

"We are putting this on a fast track because we see how very important it is to have identification as a means of being able to give support, protection and to help with order in the society,"

He urged Jamaicans, where possible, to utilise online services to minimise crowding in establishments.

"There is a cultural shift that needs to take place and we need to use this crisis to appeal to our people to use the digital platforms," the Prime Minister said.

"Many of them are not able to use digital interface, they may not be able to use the apps and the websites and some of them don't have computers to access, but when you look at the statistics showing Internet access and penetration, it is growing, but it all depends on how we, as lawmakers, signal the importance of what it means to have a digital society," he added. (Chris Patterson, April 30, 2020).

Mr. Anand Biradar, Vice President and Business Head, Hidunja Global Service, echoed similar sentiments for the continuation of the work from home strategy, which officially ends on August 31, 2020. He balanced the arguments for and against its continuation. The positives, he says, are:

1. Decreased absenteeism

2. Decreased attrition rate

3. Convenience for mothers/ families

The cons are:

1. Potential unreliability of the Internet and the electricity.

   Key to operations is the constant availability of Internet connectivity, particularly in terms of speed and spread (functioning in remote locations)

2. Opportunities for scamming and fraud.

For this element, some solutions are forthcoming. He indicated that cameras are installed at workers' homes (their workstations specifically), as they deal with sensitive personal data. He says that once the worker stops his task, the entire computer system shuts down.

He went on further to say that there are evolving data protection technologies. One he cited was where if the system detected a cellular phone that the computer screen would automatically go blank. Mr. Biradar expects implementation in months to a year.

He also mentioned the use of NFCs (Near Field Communication technology). Instead of swiping a card, the individual can put it near the system/machine, and the system/machine will then process the transaction.

Adaptation to the evolving technology is the "road we have to take" in order to remain viable players in the industry. He estimates that Jamaica would lose 30% of business if we do not adapt and if we do not continue with the work from home operation and build it as a feature in Business Continuity Plans (BCPs).

Mr. Biradar predicts that in 5-10 years BPO tasks will be done by robots, automatically, or be done by a talented human. Persons can operate from anywhere in the world on any device at any time, expanding access to available work. "The more friendly you are in terms of legislative rules and in the vehicles provided for business growth" will help to make Jamaica be fully competitive in this industry. His recommendation to put Jamaica on this trajectory for growth is to have solid Internet, a talented team, and the work from home policy. Under this policy, he estimates that 100 thousand persons will be employed. "Work from Home, and eventually Work from Anywhere is the reality of the future".

Responses to the covid crisis puts a heavy reliance on the use of technology, promotes virtual connections, and highlights the need for digital security, which eliminates individual privacy as we know it, and makes commerce and communication literally just a click away—incremental adaptations setting the stage for the New World Order.

In modern times a card has been used to store our personal information and give us ready access to funds. This card has t a built-in computer chip so once you receive that card every possible information about yourself can be brought up once it is scanned through a machine. Here is the frightening part. The latest plan is to do away with this card since it can easily be stolen or lost. They intend to replace it with a small microchip which can easily be inserted in the forehead or the hand.

This microchip or biochip will have close to an unlimited *capacity* to store information about a person, including his/her financial position. This chip is the size of a small rice grain and is easily implantable beneath the skin. The question that is begging to be asked is, "Is there such a chip in existence"? The answer is yes! In fact, the technology is perfected; and it is only a matter of time until we see full utilization. This chip will have a number for each individual and means of identifying and tracking that individual. Privacy will be a thing of the past. You will be under constant surveillance.

This system is real, and when that chip is placed beneath your skin, (in your hand or forehead) it will be the means by which commerce is approached. There will be no need for cash. Your goods are checked, your hand passed over a scanner and, the amount of funds for the goods will be automatically deducted and the transaction completed. It will mean that one will have to have his chip implanted if he is to take part in this new way of doing business transactions. Does this sound familiar?

> *"And he causes all, the small and the great, and the rich and the poor, and the freemen and the slaves, to be given a mark on their right hand or on their forehead, and he provides that no one will be able to buy or to sell, except the one who has the mark, either the name of the beast or the number of his name. Here is wisdom. Let him who has understanding calculate the number of*

> *the beast, for the number is that of a man; and his number is six hundred and sixty-six"* - Revelation 13:16-18.

The system that will usher in that terrible mark – 666 is upon us. This microchip is *already* in existence and is in use. The New York Post reported on implantation done in Sweden. The implantation was done as a measure of convenience to eliminate the need to carry cash, and multiple credit cards. It would even make easier day-to-day tasks such as opening an office or building door and monitoring one's health.

"Microchip implants are essentially cylindrical bar codes that when scanned, transmit a unique signal through a layer of skin." (Schwartz, 2019)

It is the size of a small rice grain and is easily implantable beneath the skin. The chip will have a number for each individual and means of identifying and tracking that individual. Privacy will be a thing of the past. The 'chipped' individual will be under constant surveillance.

Let us read excerpts of this article written on July 18, 2019: **_Everything you need to know before getting an RFID implant._** (https://medicalfuturist.com/rfid-implant-chip/).

The radio-frequency-identification (RFID) technology has been around for decades. It is a tag, label or card that can exchange data with a reader using radio frequency (RF) signals. It usually has a built-in antenna and an integrated circuit (IC). The RFID chip is a bar code label as it also typically works with a scanner or reader, although it has a wider scope. You can use it for almost anything: clothes, shoes, vehicles, animals, and even people.

RFID chips as luggage tags make sure that your suitcase arrives where it was supposed to go. [You] *probably already have a personal RFID chip that goes with you everywhere.* It's in your credit card. The first-ever human to receive an RFID microchip implant was British scientist Kevin Warwick (known by the moniker "Captain Cyborg") in 1998. This experiment allowed a computer to monitor Warwick as he moved through halls and offices of the Department of Cybernetics at the University of Reading, using a unique identifying signal emitted by the implanted chip. He could operate doors, lights, heaters, and other computers without lifting a finger. Approximately two decades later, the technology had been made commercially available, and thousands of people decided to implant an RFID chip.

For example, groups of people have been meeting at "implant parties," often organized by larger companies, to hook themselves up. They are especially popular in Sweden, where more than

4,000 individuals can take pride in opening doors with only lifting their hands.

In the future, an RFID chip implanted into your hand, between your thumb and your index finger on the back of your hand, could contain a lot of useful information – that you usually carry around in your wallet or purse. It can <u>transmit your identity information as you walk through a security checkpoint</u> enable you to use public transport and make long lines at the supermarket checkout a thing of the past. You will never have to worry about losing your most important documents or your wallet ever again – and 'within hand's reach' will most certainly have a second layer of meaning to it.

Moreover, imagine that in a medical emergency, the first responders will only have to scan your hand to get to know every valuable bit of medical data about you.

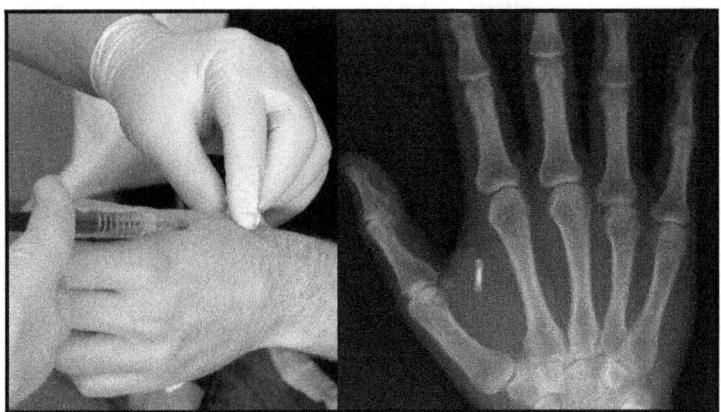

The Anatomy of the RFID Chip

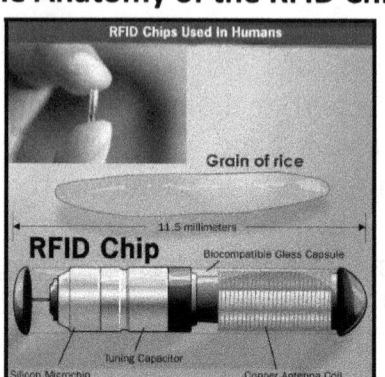

https://i.pinimg.com/originals/51/b7/fb/51b7fbdc99beac3d5e7e9246be322db7.jpg

This system to make all of these things possible is now here with the unveiling of what is called the 5G network. Possibly, the ultimate in facilitating communication technology. Yes folks, the system is literal and is very real and when that chip is placed beneath your skin (in your hand or in your forehead) it will be the means by which commerce is approached in the future.

There is no need for cash. Your goods are checked, your hand passed over a scanner and, the amount for the goods *automatically* deducted and transaction completed. One will have to have this chip implanted in order to take part in this new way of doing business transactions.

It means an individual in the future will be unable to transact business without this facility (in the same way that a person in Jamaica cannot now insure etc. his/her vehicle unless they have their TRN number).

On January 30, 2018, an article entitled <u>The New National Identification Systems</u>, with the focus on the USA revealed that the, "REAL ID Act (Federal Law), passed in 2005, [sought] to subject state drivers' licensing to federal data collection and information - sharing standards that will facilitate identification and tracking.

State promotion of the E-Verify background check system, which is intended to control the employment of illegal immigrants, is another path to a national ID.

This paper summarizes the stances of each of the 50 states on various ID systems, including REAL ID, E-Verify, facial recognition, and license - plate scanning.

Together, those technologies—along with other initiatives orchestrated at the federal level - are the leading edge of a national identification and tracking infrastructure." (Harper, 2018)

The advances in technology and the need for comprehensive information on individuals give us a clear signal of how things will be done in the future. There will ultimately be a storehouse of records of all individuals with details of everything about them. Governments, for example, posit that this information can assist in national development planning and security. Privacy will be no more. Personal lives will be an accessible open book.

All of us know about the United Nations (UN). It is that one body which spans every country of the world. On the seat of this body sits the USA, Russia, Red China and the great European powers; as well as countries from poor and developing regions. This body can pass resolutions to enable a country to be attacked by others (as in the case of Iraq) or to be delivered (as in the case of Kuwait). The UN will be playing an important role in this one world government programme that will be the hallmark of the Antichrist's reign Just how could the United Nations play a part in these end time events?

You may be surprised to know the following facts:

The United Nations, though accepted by many as a body that brings the nations of this earth together, does not have a constitution to guide how it should carry out its mandate! They have what is called a UN Charter, but this is not a constitution. There is a document already in circulation to different nations which is a draft constitution for the UN. This document is called, **"A Constitution for the Federation of Earth"**. This is literally bringing the nations of earth together to form a single body. Could it be a mere coincidence that the logo or symbol of the Council for Foreign Relation (CFR) in the UN is a man riding on a white horse? You judge for yourself.

This coming New World Order is practically here. Indeed, this universally dramatic change in the accepted norm, in terms of relations among nations, is being implemented at break-neck speed.

Economies around the world are integrating. A problem in one nation, can impact all other nations around because of how deep and entrenched are the economies of the nation states. The book of Revelation is unfolding before our very eyes ladies and gentlemen.

In closing this section, let me share with you an additional piece of information about how factual and real this coming New World Order really is.

If you have a US$1.00 bill, look at the back of it to the left-hand corner. There is a symbol of a pyramid with a human eye at the apex. Around that symbol are the Latin words:

Annuit Coeptis Novus Ordo Sellorum.

Translating that into English reads, *"Announcing the birth of the New World Order".*

https://st2.depositphotos.com/4225551/6582/i/950/depositphotos_65823651-stock-photo-one-us-dollar-banknote-back.jpg

One thing is certain, the days are moving fast, and the night is at hand. The fact is it is one minute to midnight.

CHAPTER 4

ONE WORLD RELIGION AND THE NEW AGE MOVEMENT

The Bible speaks about the establishment of a global religious system in the end-times. The elements of this system are coming together before our very eyes after going through a number of iterations over the years. At this point in our history, we are seeing the most recognisable religious leader in the world, the Pope, asking religious leaders in and out of Christendom to put aside certain things in our Christian beliefs so that there can be a unified religious order going forward. The broad objective is to unite all the religious groupings across the world into one entity, and this will be achieved under the aegis of tolerance. The basic script is – let us put aside the belief systems, certain doctrine that we adhere to that could exclude others (doctrines like, I am the way the truth and the life, no man cometh unto the father but through me i.e. Jesus – my interpretation), and let us unite with what is common to all, that is, our common humanity.

Also, in other quarters there are calls to unite since we all believe in a god and have a common desire to want to serve this particular god. They make the point that it should not matter who that god is, so long as there is a genuine desire to serve this being. In this way no one is excluded, and we can achieve religious inclusion for all, and therefore we can all unite and work together under one body, looking to one God; whomever we make out that god to be. Who or what you believe in should not matter at all.

Brothers and sisters, we are marching straight into this scenario right now. All the elements of a global and united religious system are converging right now. The push for inter-faith and ecumenical integration is at a peak right now, even to the point where it is taking on threatening tones. We will see more of this as we read further and get to the section on the New Age Movement.

Mr. Robert Muller, a former Assistant Secretary to the United Nations made very profound statements regarding the formation of a one world religious organisation. The very thing that was predicted by the Apostle John to come on stream in the end of days. Revelation 13:16-18,

In a piece written in the **World Business Academy**, September 29, 2005, Vol. 19, Issue 8, entitled *Proper Earth Government: A framework and ways to create it*; Muller expressed a concern that religions did not globalise themselves. He further expressed that religions still believed that their truths were absolute, immortal and meant to be spread to the entire world. See how this opposes the words of the Lord Jesus,

"**Go ye therefore and teach all nations**...-.Matthew 28:19-20.

Unbelievable!

He went on further, "Today our objectives and efforts must be: to see the religions globalise themselves into a global spiritual renaissance, in order to give us a universal, cosmic meaning of life on earth and give birth to the first global, cosmic, universal civilisation. The United Religions Organisation which is in the process of being created can do that".

It has been put forward that the world is now being brought together as far as possible, politically. However, to have a true world government it has to be brought together spiritually.

The Bible was spot on. The Antichrist and the false prophet (the leader of this one world religious body which deceived many) works hand in hand to accomplish their diabolical plans. Let us look at the following extracts….

Pope Francis to world's religious leaders: We build the future together or there will be no future

Gerard O'Connell February 04, 2019

"There is no alternative: We either build the future together or there will not be a future," Pope Francis said frankly in an important keynote address to participants at the high-level interreligious meeting in Abu Dhabi on Feb. 4.

"Religions, in particular, cannot renounce the urgent task of building bridges between peoples and cultures," he told the 700 representatives of Islam, Christianity, Judaism and other religions at an open-air gathering at the memorial to the founding father of the United Arab Emirates.

"The time has come when religions should more actively exert themselves, with courage and audacity and without pretence, to help the human family deepen the capacity for reconciliation, the vision of hope and the concrete paths of peace," Pope Francis said.

Drawing on this image, Pope Francis told his interreligious audience: "Today, we too in the name of God, in order to safeguard peace, need to enter together as one family into an ark which can sail the stormy seas of the world: the ark of fraternity."

He insisted that "each belief system is called to overcome the divide between friends and enemies, in order to take up the perspective of heaven, which embraces persons without privilege or discrimination."

While this is forging ahead full speed, there is within this religious group that parades as a "Christian group". This group is called the New Age Movement.

> **"But *evil men and seducers shall wax worse and worse, deceiving and being deceived*"** – 2 Timothy 3:13.

The new agers are associated with a religious group that has a worldwide agenda of converting men to a form of spiritual experience based upon a religion known as, Spiritism.

This form of worship has serious aspects of devil worship, which the unsuspecting individual knows nothing about. Yet, although there are some very unsettling rituals and chants involved; people somehow still become attracted to it and ultimately become new agers themselves.

This religion is one of the fastest growing movement in the world today. It has infiltrated every sphere of society and is being promoted in books, music, on television and all over society.

The frightening thing about this movement is that many of its adherents profess Christianity. The unsuspecting Christian may, therefore, be led astray quite easily by books or sermons delivered by these people.

Some of them are well-known personalities in Christian circles. We therefore need to heed the warnings of the apostles of old:

> ***"But though we, or an angel from heaven, preach any other gospel unto you than that which we have preached unto you, let him be accursed"*** Galatians 1:8.

True Christians will have to take their stance where the gospel of Jesus Christ is concerned. The Word of God makes it explicitly clear that, **"I am the way, the truth and the life, no man comes to the Father but through Me"** John 14:6. It also describes him as:

- The Door (St John 10:9)
- The Resurrection and the Life (St John 11:25)
- The Light of the World (St John 8:12)
- The Bread of Life (St. John 6: 35)
- The Good Shepherd (St. John 10: 11)

This means that there is absolutely no way (religious or otherwise), that mankind can have true fellowship and communion with Almighty God, *except* through Jesus Christ.

> *"Neither is there salvation in any other: for there is none other name under heaven given among men, whereby we must be saved"* Acts 4:12.

> And, this…*"If anyone comes to you and does not bring this teaching, do not receive him into your house, and do not greet him"* - 2 John 10.

As Christians, we must teach and preach these truths. New agers, however, think differently and make it quite clear just what they think about us, as Christians.

They say that the born-again Christians who hold to these things stated above, are negative and are responsible for animosity among different religious groups.

As a result, there are some serious comments made about true children of God that are very frightening. I quote the word of some prominent leaders of the New Age Movement as they describe certain Christians:

"The fundamentalist Christians are the worst Christians. They are the most fanatical people. They believe that Christianity is the only religion. All other religions are wrong, and they believe that the world should be turned towards Christianity. These are very primitive ideas." (OSHO, p. 125).

As a result of holding to these views, Christians are hated by many in the New Age Movement. It has reached the point where very serious statements have been made about getting rid of fundamentalist Christians.

Djwhal Khul, another leader of this movement has this to say in reference to Christians,

"The foetus of the new humanity is already stirring in the womb of time and like the human mother, humanity must learn to eliminate its waste materials and poisons."

What is he saying?

This new humanity is referring to a reorganization of the religious order as we know it.

It is already in the making and whatever it is that stands in the way of it coming forth, must be eliminated, just as waste materials and poisons are eliminated from the body.

Again, another significant statement by the same person relating to Christians:

>**"Another surgical operation may be necessary to dissipate this infection and get rid of the fever."**

This is simply referring to a medical surgeon carrying out an operation and cutting off the entire infected area to get rid of the cause of the problem.

These are profound statements, and there have been many more said that contain serious charges.

This group is pushing for Christianity to embrace other religious bodies to form a unified group seeking to please the same one creator, or so they claim.

Everyone knows the Lord's Prayer. This godly prayer was taught to us by Jesus and was recorded in Matthews 6:9-13.

In it we literally request of the Lord for His Kingdom to come and that *His* will be done on earth, as it is in heaven.

You may be surprised to know that the New Age Movement has its *own* prayer of sort. They call it The Great Invocation.

It goes like this:

> *"Let the lords of liberation issue forth. Let the rider from the secret place come forth, and coming, save. Come forth, O mighty one. Let light and love and power and death fulfil the purpose of the coming one."*

The "coming one" that they are requesting to arrive is certainly *not* Jesus Christ, it is none other than the Antichrist himself, the Beast that we spoke about in Chapter Two.

The real plan of the New Age Movement is to achieve religious world unity. But now we need to acknowledge something far scarier, that they are planning for a one-world head of this unified religious order.

Apart from a One-World Government, there is to be a one-world church or religious group to be the hub of unity of religious bodies.

This process is taking longer because some Christians continue to maintain that they will *not* join forces with other religions bodies in pursuit of this one universal religions system.

Some of these leaders go as far as falsely claiming how 'closely-knit' Christianity is with ancient Eastern religious.

Clearly those in this group are becoming increasingly frustrated with those Christians who are holding on to the belief that Jesus Christ is the *only* way to salvation.

Can we then begin to understand why Christians are increasingly coming under persecution worldwide?

Open Doors USA

A community of Christians who come together to support persecuted believers, have indicated that there is a growing trend in Christian persecution across many countries. They have reported that over 260 million Christians are living in places where they experience high levels of persecution.

They have shown where many Christians are killed for their faith, churches and other Christian buildings attacked. Believers detained without trial, arrested and sentenced. These are things happening right now in countries like Pakistan, North Korea, Somalia, Libya, and Afghanistan. It is actually bordering on genocide in some places. In 2018 alone it is reported that some 400 Christians were murdered for their faith.

This does not consider the shift in the USA for example, which was once considered a Christian country. Now, the Bible is banned from school, prayer is banned from public places, Christians and Christian organisations are under constant scrutiny.

There is indeed a shift and we better wake up to this reality and also know that it is getting progressively worse.

Keep holding on, dear brothers and sisters! As Christians, our faith is in the Word of God.

The Bible dispenses the truths of the living God by which we live our lives daily, and it is in those sacred pages that we *know* what is in store for us when this life is over.

The New Agers have their own bibles, like the satanic bible or one known as the Aquarian Gospel of Jesus Christ. Here is a note for your information:

The leaders of this movement after carefully planning and organizing their goals; have established a target date for fully embracing the New Age Movement, and the revelation of a new period which they call, The Age of Aquarius.

CHAPTER 5

END TIME CALENDAR
(Daniel's 70 Weeks)

The Babylonian Empire was the greatest in antiquity. Led by King Nebuchadnezzar, they overthrew the nation of Israel and took captive some of the most brilliant of the Israelites, to integrate them into the Babylonian system as advisors and consultants. Amongst those taken captive was a young man named Daniel. This young man stood out because of his genuine character and the spirit of excellence that evidently characterized his life. God had bestowed on him a tremendous prophetic gift which was observed by the Babylonian elites, and in the course of time Daniel, the captive, was elevated to become the chief minister in Babylon. Possibly only a very small handful of men equalled him in terms of his authority and influence.

Amongst those left back in Jerusalem was Jeremiah, the prophet. He continued as a prophet of the Most High God and prophesied to the remainder of the Jews still living in Jerusalem under the Babylonian occupation. Jeremiah prophesied that they shall serve the king of Babylon seventy years. Jeremiah 25:11 ***"And this whole land shall be a desolation, and an astonishment; and these nations shall serve the King of Babylon seventy years"***.

It was now about sixty-eight years that Daniel was in captivity, and he read the prophetic writings of

Jeremiah and recognized that the seventy years of the captivity would soon come to an end. As a result of this, Daniel began to seek the face of the Lord for the future of his people.

> *"In the first year of Darius the son of Ahasuerus, of the seed of the Medes, which was made King over the realm of the Chaldeans; in the first year of his reign I Daniel understood by books the number of the years, whereof the word of the Lord came to Jeremiah the prophet, that he would accomplish seventy years in the desolations of Jerusalem"*, Daniel 9:1-2

It was in this time of prayer and seeking God that the angel Gabriel appeared to him and began to outline the prophecy of the seventy weeks, after giving him "skill and understanding" with regards to future events - Daniel 9:24-27.

It is important now to hear and understand the words of this prophecy. God, in these scriptures, gives us a panorama of the events that will take us right down to the closing of the curtains on planet earth—the end of time. *"Seventy weeks are determined (destined) upon thy people and upon thy holy city, to finish the transgression, and to make an end of sins, and to make reconciliation for iniquity, and to bring in everlasting righteousness, and to seal up the vision and prophecy, and to anoint the most Holy"*, Daniel 9:24.

Notice that the prophecy is focused on Daniel's people and the city. This means it is centred around the children of Israel and the city of Jerusalem. Although the things contained herein will impact all the nations of the world, God literally has everything pivoted around his people, Israel.

If we are therefore to understand end-time things, we must understand the prophecy of Daniel's seventy weeks and recognize that the nation of Israel has a role in end time events. We will look at this in a section of the last chapter.

In these seventy-weeks, God will realign everything back into the order and balance that He has determined and decreed. God is executing His purpose and plans, totally unmoved by all the other things that are advancing in world affairs.

It is important to point out that the seventy weeks does not run straight from week one to week seventy.

We will see that there will be an interruption somewhere in the span of the seventy-week period – Daniel 9:25-26:

> *"Know therefore and understand, that from the going forth of the commandment to restore and to build Jerusalem unto the Messiah the Prince shall be seven weeks, and threescore and*

> *two weeks: the street shall be built again, and the wall, even in troublous times.*
>
> *And after threescore and two weeks shall Messiah be cut off, but not for himself: and the people of the prince that shall come shall destroy the city and the sanctuary; and the end thereof shall be with a flood, and unto the end of the war desolations are determined".*

Sixty-nine of the weeks will pass and then something significant happens. Messiah, the Prince shall come and shall be cut off (but not for himself). This Messiah of Israel, and for us (Gentiles), the Saviour of the world, was cut off, that is, killed. Notice that something significant happens as a result of this. The prophetic clock for Israel stops. So, at the sixty-ninth week, there is a stand-still in terms of the counting, and something happened that was never seen by any of the Old Testament prophets.

This period at the end of the sixty-ninth week, and before the seventieth week is characterized by a body called 'The Church'. It is here that Gentiles (dogs, the degenerate and filthy, as Gentiles were described), if they believed and accepted the Gospel message, can come into right relationship with Almighty God.

This is what is happening from the time that Jesus was crucified, right up to this very point today: the Lord is calling out of the Gentiles a people for His name – Acts 15:14 "….. *how God at the first did visit the Gentiles, to take out of them a people for His name"*.

At the end of this period (between the sixty-ninth and seventieth week), the 'Church' period, the Church will be raptured (caught away), and the prophetic clock (for Israel) which had stopped, will again start ticking, and that last week, the 70th week, begins.

> "*…..that blindness in part is happened to Israel, until the fulness of the Gentiles be come in",* Romans 11:25

It continues God's cycle with Israel.

This last week, also called the 'time of Jacob's trouble' – Jeremiah 30:7. :*'Alas! For that day is great, so that none is like it: it is even the time of Jacob's trouble, but he shall be saved out of it'*. Read also Matthew 24:15-31.

It is at the time of the Rapture, after the Church has left, that the prophetic clock starts ticking again and we resume counting for that final week in Daniel's prophecy. Remember that up to the time that Messiah was cut off, we had only reached sixty-nine weeks of Daniel's seventy weeks prophecy.

The Bible is clear as to what will unfold in this last week of the prophecy. The same Daniel told us that God would confirm the covenant for one week (seven years). This period (one week) represents the last leg of the seventy weeks prophecy, and Daniel saw right down to this time.

It is important to discuss here the meaning of the term 'weeks' as seen in the scriptures, so that we can properly understand the prophecy and establish the time sequencing.

In our western (English) culture, when we speak of 'weeks', we automatically assume a period of seven days. The Hebrew use of the word is different from the general English use however. This was stated earlier in the chapter.

Daniel, recognising that according to Jeremiah's prophecy that the end of the seventy years were drawing near, started to seek the face of the Lord. If we look well, we will see that Daniel was thinking in terms of years and not days. Let us dig deeper as we try to understand what is being conveyed here.

The Hebrew word translated weeks is *'Shabua'*, and it means 'a seven'.

So, Daniel 9:24 literally says, "**Seventy sevens** ……."

These are weeks of years and not weeks of days. A seven represents a period of seven years, so that the scripture above which states 'seventy sevens', would be 490 years (70x7) and not 490 weeks.

Let us use the Bible itself to prove this point. We will examine a well-known scripture to establish the point. It shows the use of the word 'weeks' to represent a seven-year period.

> *"And Laban said, it must not be so done in our country, to give the younger before the first born. Fulfil her <u>week</u> and we will give thee this also for the service which thou shalt serve with me yet seven other years. And Jacob did so and fulfilled her week: and he gave him Rachel, his daughter to wife also",* Genesis 29:26-28

We all know from the scriptures Jacob had to work 14 years for Rachel. Yet it is described here as him having to fulfil her **week** so that he could have Rachel whom he really loved.

It is the same Hebrew word *'Shabua'* that is used here, which is used in Daniel's seventy weeks. So, it is clear that he is speaking in terms of years and not days. In this context therefore, a 'seven' is a period of seven years. Compare this to our western culture where we say a decade is a period of ten years - same concept.

Therefore, seventy decades would be 70x10, that is seven hundred years. In the same way, seventy sevens would be 70x7, that is four hundred and ninety years.

So, God was saying to Daniel that there is going to be a 490-year period in which I (the Lord) am going to accomplish some things to achieve my purpose in relation to my people Israel.

According to Daniel 9:24, there are six things that need to happen in this time-period to fulfil God's purpose over his people and usher in the final things.

The Word said, ***"Seventy weeks are determined upon thy people ...."*** to:

Finish the transgression.

Their (Israel's) act of rebellion and rejection of their Messiah represents a transgression passed down to their children. Within the timeframe of this 490-year period, there will come a time when the Jews will recognize Jesus as their Messiah and accept Him as such.

At this point of acknowledgement and acceptance, the transgression will be finished.

> *"And the Redeemer shall come to Zion, and unto them that turn from transgression in Jacob, saith the Lord. As for me, this is my covenant with them, saith the Lord; My spirit that is upon thee, and my words which I have put in thy mouth, shall not depart out of thy mouth, nor out of the mouth of thy seed,*

> *nor out of the mouth of thy seed's seed, saith the Lord, from henceforth and forever"* – Isaiah 59:20-21,

This, as we will see, will happen in the final week of the seventy weeks.

To make an end of sin

The history of the nation of Israel has been one of continual departure from serving their one true God. Today they serve Him, tomorrow they depart from Him and serve Baal or some other god. A day is coming however, when they (Israel) as a nation will turn to their God, never again to follow after strange gods.

> *"Plead with your mother, plead: for she is not my wife, neither am I her husband: let her therefore put away her whoredoms out of her sight, and her adulteries from between her breasts; Lest I strip her naked, and set her as in the day that she was born, and make her as a wilderness, and set her like a dry land, and slay her with thirst. And I will not have mercy upon her children; for they be children of whoredoms. For their mother hath played the harlot: she that conceived them hath done shamefully: for she said, I will go after my lovers, that give me my bread and my water, my wool and my flax, mine oil and my drink",* Hosea 2:2-5

To make reconciliation for iniquity

There will come a point in the life of Israel when as a nation they will collectively recognize what they did when they rejected Jesus Christ, their Messiah. This realization will ultimately result in them reconciling to God as they recognize that this Jesus was indeed their long-awaited Messiah whom they had crucified.

The Lord will be merciful to them, of course, and there will be national reconciliation.

> *"In those days, and in that time, saith the Lord, the iniquity of Israel shall be sought for, and there shall be none; and the sins of Judah, and they shall not be found: for I will pardon them whom I reserve",* Jeremiah 50:20.

Bring in everlasting righteousness

With this seventy weeks (seven) period, a time will come where righteousness will radiate from sea to shining sea. This speaks to the establishment of the long-awaited Millennial Kingdom and afterwards, when the Lord shall be King over all the earth, in that day shall there be one Lord, and His name one. See Isaiah 11:1, 4-6; 32:16-19; Zechariah 14:9.

To seal up the vision and prophecy

Seal up means 'to complete', 'to cease', 'to bring to an end'. All the visions given to holy men of old, and

words of prophecy committed to them in relation to the coming of Christ and the Kingdom, would have found their fulfilment.

There will certainly not be the need any more for prophets and prophecies, in that all that the prophets spoke about in terms of the Christ and the Kingdom would have been fulfilled. Genesis 3:15, "*And I will put enmity between thee and the woman he said, I will greatly multiply thy sorrow and thy conception; in sorrow thou shalt bring forth children; and thy desire shall be to thy husband, and he shall rule over thee*", would have had its fulfilment at Calvary and finally at the establishment of the Kingdom here on earth, with the binding of Satan and ultimately his demise.

To anoint the Most Holy

Anointing the Most Holy can refer to a number of things: the Holy of Holies in the temple, the temple itself was referred to as such, the vessels within the body of holiness, or even the priests themselves.

Let us just look at the seventy weeks and how it is broken down according to the scriptures, and then fit everything together. In other words, when does it begin and by extension when does it end?

> Daniel 9:25, **"Know therefore and understand that from the going forth of the commandment to restore and to build Jerusalem, unto the Messiah the Prince, shall be seven weeks, and three score and two weeks...."**
>
> Verse 26: **"And after threescore and two weeks shall Messiah be cut off...."**
>
> Verse 27: **"And he shall confirm the covenant with many for one week ...."**

There were a number of decrees issued in relation to the restoration of the temple and it is therefore important that we properly identify which one would constitute the commencement of the seventy weeks prophecy.

Recall the decrees by Darius, Cyrus, and Artaxerxes. All these decrees were in relation to the rebuilding of the temple. However, the prophecy gives the timing as from the going forth of the commandment to restore and to build Jerusalem. That is the key.

The only command in connection to Jerusalem was by King Artaxerxes, which is found in Nehemiah 1:1-4 and Nehemiah 2:1-8. We now need to be clear on the particular date, and we will be in a position to properly do the count for the starting time for the seventy weeks. The answer to this is in verse 1 of Nehemiah chapter 2. Nehemiah stated that the decree was issued in the month of Nissan in the 20th year of the Artaxerxes. This king began his reign 465BC and so twenty years into his reign would be 445BC. Notice also that Nehemiah only said the month of Nissan, without giving a particular date. Jewish customunderstands that when no date is given, it is taken as the first day of the month. Given the above, we know therefore that the seventy weeks began on 1st Nissan 445 BC.

We said earlier that the seventy weeks are broken down into segments.

> Daniel 9:25, *"**Know therefore and understand that from the going forth of the commandment to restore and to build Jerusalem shall be <u>seven weeks</u>**"*.

Watch again.

> Daniel 9:26, *"**And after three score and two weeks shall Messiah be cut off……**"*

Notice that the seventy weeks are broken down into periods of time – seven weeks, and then **threescore and two weeks**. That first period of seven weeks (49 years) represented the time that the restoration of Jerusalem took. This corroborates with secular history which recorded that the rebuilding of the city took approximately 50 years.

Then the second period picks up immediately at the completion of the first and runs for sixty-two weeks (439 years). At the end of this period, Messiah the Prince was cut off (killed). This represents the time of crucifixion of Jesus Christ, the Messiah that the Jews rejected and killed. The first two periods within the seventy weeks (i.e. seven weeks – (49 years) and sixty-two weeks (434 years) came to a close.

Here now is a point that is so crucial, and which shows the power of this seventy weeks prophecy by Daniel, which many miss. The counting of the seventy years begins at 1st Nissan 445BC. So far, we have seen that there were two periods within this span of time: the first period of seven weeks (49 years) and the second period of sixty-two weeks (434 years). This accounts for sixty-nine weeks (483 years) that is (7 weeks + 62 weeks = 69 weeks).

After Messiah was cut off, (not for himself), the Church came into being. The prophecy clock stopped ticking. Thus, there is a gap between the 69th week and the 70th week. The prophets of old did not see this gap: this body of "called out believers', this act of God calling the "Gentiles, a people for His name".

We are still in this gap period—the Church Age. The scriptures describe it this way, *"blindness in part is happened to Israel until the fulness of Gentiles be come in"*. Let us look at what happened. Jesus rode into Jerusalem on one fateful day on an ass exactly as it was prophesied in Zechariah 9:9. The disciples, and I would imagine a few others, recognized him as the Messiah and there was a mini celebration as he rode in:

> Luke 19:38, *"Saying, Blessed be the King that cometh in the name of the Lord: peace in heaven, and glory in the highest"*.

Notice what Jesus had earlier said as he stood and looked over Jerusalem and wept.

> Luke 9:41-44 – *"if thou hadst known, even thou, at least in this thy day, the things which belong unto thy peace. But now they are hid from thine eyes. For the days shall come upon thee, that thine enemies shall cast a trench about thee, and compass thee round, and keep thee in on every side, and shall lay these even with the ground, and thy children within thee; and they shall not leave in thee one stone upon another; because thou knewest not the time of thy visitation"*.

Notice Jesus' words about Jerusalem – *"**If thou hadst known, even thou, at least <u>in this thy day</u>…..**"* What was so special about this day? It was their day to decide, the *"time of their visitation"*. Would they accept Jesus or deny him as their Messiah? They rejected him that day. A couple days later Jesus was crucified.

The promised Kingdom on earth, with Jesus Christ the Messiah as King, was now on hold. It is still on hold while the Lord is working with the Church.

Earlier on I said that there was something that many people missed. A point that I believe is significant. We already showed the breakdown of the seventy weeks and showed that we went up to the 69th week, and then the prophecy clock stopped ticking. Now 69 weeks equates to 483 years. We showed earlier how we would compute this. Now there are 360 days in the Hebrew calendar and not 365 as in our Julian calendar. So, if we want to look at the 69 weeks, which is 483 years and then bring that to days, we can. It is simply multiplying 360 days x 483 years = 173,880 days. Something very serious and interesting emerges when we start counting from 1st Nissan BC., and count 173,880 days (which is 69 weeks). It lands exactly on April 6, 33 AD. This was a Sunday, the very Sunday before his crucifixion. This was therefore Palm Sunday, the very day that they were spreading their clothes on the ground and spreading palm leaves on the ground for Jesus as he rode on the ass into Jerusalem. Yet it was on this very day, they rejected him and started to shout later, crucify him. This was the very day of the rejection of Messiah. Within five days of this, Messiah was crucified (cut off) according to the prophecy. "......*after threescore and two weeks shall Messiah be cut off*", Daniel 9:25-26.

Final Week of the Prophecy

We know from scriptures that the prophecy is for seventy weeks. This as we already see was broken down into sections - the first being seven weeks (7 x 7 = 49 years), the second was sixty-two weeks (62 x 7 = 434 years). There was then a gap period, where the Church emerged. The prophecy time clock for Israel had stopped ticking.

The prophecy however is for seventy weeks. There is therefore a one-week period (1 x 7 = 7 years) that is required to complete the seventy weeks.

See the three periods outlined in summary:

1st seven weeks (sevens)   - (7 x 7 years = 49 years)

2nd sixty-two weeks (sevens)   - (62 x7 years = 434 years)

3rd one week (sevens) - (1 x 7 years = 7 years)

We saw that the first two went together and related to the rebuilding of the city of Jerusalem and to the cutting off of Messiah the Prince, Jesus Christ. At this point we are in the Church Age. So, we are left with the final period of one week.

> Daniel 9:27, *"**And he shall confirm the covenant with many for one week: and in***

the midst of the week he shall cause the sacrifice and the oblation to cease ...."

At this point in time, the Church Age would have been finished. The Rapture would have taken place, and God would then turn again to complete His programme with

Israel. Remember, *'blindness in part is happened to Israel until the fulness of the gentiles be come in'*.

The fullness of the Gentiles has to do with the Church period and represents that time after the end of the Church Age when God again deals with Israel as a nation.

In returning his attention to Israel, and in dealing with them according to the seventy weeks prophecy that He gave to Daniel, there was one week to go to complete that which is determined. It is this one week (7 years) that we generally refer to as the Tribulation Period. It is described in Jeremiah 30:7 as the 'time of Jacob's trouble', giving us the clear understanding that it essentially has to do with Israel.

The things that will characterize this final one week (seven years) will be:

- The rise of the Antichrist. He actually will forge a covenant (agreement) with Israel that will be recognized as a tremendous accomplishment. In the midst of the week he will break it and move to install himself as Israel's Messiah.

- The pouring out of the judgements or wrath of God upon inhabitants of earth, by way of:

  ❖ The seven seal judgements
  ❖ The seven trumpet judgements
  ❖ The seven vials judgements
  ❖ The New World Order to include the Mark of the Beast, etc.

At the end of that seven year period, however, Jesus will return to this earth again with the saints, Jude 14; Rev. 19:15, and he (Jesus) shall stand in that day upon the Mount of Olives - Zechariah 14:9.

After engaging in the Battle of Armageddon (read more in Chapter 7), He will move to establish the millennial kingdom here on earth, and thereafter the eternal state (ie. heaven), thus fulfilling to the maximum, the prophecies of Daniel 70 weeks.

CHAPTER 6

THE RAPTURE

When we look at the headlines in papers across the world, there is certainly the feeling of gloom, despair, and despondency. Some are literally pushed into depression. Consider the Covid-19 today. Earlier we had AIDS, Ebola, SARS, H1N1. All these headlines leave a sense of foreboding, and no hope for the future. In addition to what is happening, and what we are seeing in past headlines, there is the reality facing us in terms of what is next to come.

Together these things present a frightening picture and gives us a feel of helplessness and loss. Yet, in the midst of such uncertainties there are a group of people that are anxiously and passionately looking and longing for an event that represents one of the crowning features in the life of the child of God. This event is the 'Rapture of the Church'.

It is the moment when according to 1 Thess. 4:16,

> *"...the Lord himself shall descend from heaven with a shout, with the voice of the archangel, and with the trump of God: and the dead in Christ shall rise first. Then we which are alive and remain shall be caught up together with them in the clouds, to meet the Lord in the air: and so, shall we ever be with the Lord".*

This event where the saints of God are literally caught up to meet the Lord Jesus in the clouds and be escorted by Him into heaven is the rapture. Oh! What a blessed hope it is for those who believe and trust in the Lord Jesus.

The Apostle Paul spoke further and gave additional details about this event when he wrote to the church of Corinth in 1 Cor. 15:51-53. He says,

> *"Behold, I shew you a mystery; we shall not all sleep, but we shall all be changed, in a moment in the twinkling of an eye at the last trump. For the trumpet shall sound and the dead shall be raised incorruptible and we shall be changed. For this corruptible must put on incorruption and this mortal must put on immortality".*

These scriptures together, give us the basic order of this great and imminent event. First, the Lord will descend from heaven with a loud and authoritative shout. It is interesting to note that He is in heaven at this very time doing amongst other things, preparing a place for us. Remember He comforted His disciples in St. John 14:2 & 3 where He said,

> *"I go to prepare a place for you and if I go and prepare a place for you, I will come again and receive you unto myself that where I am there ye may be also".*

Secondly, He will raise up those that have died and give them resurrection (glorified) bodies. Those that are alive will be changed instantly into their resurrected (glorified) bodies.

Thirdly, together we will be caught up to meet Him in the clouds and He then will escort us back to heaven with Him. This is a physical, literal event. We presently have bodies and so did Jesus. When Jesus was resurrected and clothed with his glorified body, he was still recognizable, he still ate and drank, those around could still touch him. Thus, although a spiritual working took place, the event is literal and we will just like Jesus, be clothed with glorified bodies.

> *"For our conversation is in heaven; from whence also we look for the Saviour, the Lord Jesus Christ: who shall change our vile body, that it may be fashioned like unto his glorious body, according to the working whereby he is able even to subdue all things unto himself"* Philippians 3:20-21.

This body that we have cannot go into the new heavenly realm, because it is corruptible. That means it is subject to decay, rot, degeneration etc. Thank God for the mystery that was revealed where this corruptible will be changed and become incorruptible. This means never to rot, never to be sick again. We will not only be clothed with incorruptible bodies, but these new bodies will also be clothed with immortality. So, we will never again die. No more pain, no more heartache. This is precisely what we can draw from the scriptures in 1 Corinthians 15. All this takes place at the rapture of the Church.

It is a beautiful study to examine and see that this entire sequence is reflected in the stages in a Jewish marriage ceremony in the time of Jesus. We will look at the details of this in a little while. Just to make the point here though, that this entire rapture event was detailed in the plan of God from the very beginning by way of the Jewish marriage customs which Jesus used as an analogy for this event.

Now the word *'rapture'* is not in the English translation of the Bible. It is clearly stated however in the Latin Vulgate. This is the Canon that was used for hundreds of years before the English translation. The English word *'rapture'* comes from the Latin word *'rapere'* which means to *'snatch away'* or to *'carry off'* or *'to carry away'*. So technically speaking, the word 'rapture' was always there.

The Greek word is *'harpazo'* meaning *'to carry off forcefully'*. So, in the scriptures in 1 Thess. 4 that we read earlier, the words *'caught up'* is the English translation from this Greek word, and conveys being raptured, being carried away, being caught up. Although the description of being immediately taken out of this world seems difficult to fathom, there are precedents in scriptures for such an event. The bible describes Enoch as a man whose way pleased God and the Lord took him.

> ***"And Enoch walked with God; and he was not; for God took him",*** Genesis 5:2.

> ***" By faith Enoch was translated that he should not see death; AND WAS NOT FOUND, BECAUSE GOD HAD TRANSLATED HIM: for before his translation he had this testimony, that he pleased God",*** Hebrews 11:5.

Note:

The NLT version reads "…**He disappeared**…"

The NASB version reads "…**God took him up**…"

The NIV version reads "…**God had taken him away**…"

These are the very phrases and terms used today in describing the event of the rapture. The prophet Elijah experienced a similar event, in that he did not die but was taken up to heaven, 2 Kings 2:1 & 11. One moment Elisha was walking with Elijah and then suddenly an event (a chariot of fire appeared) and separated Elisha from Elijah. One taken, the other left. Verse 12 said of Elisha, he saw him (Elijah) no more.

This understanding of Jesus rapturing the Church at any time was always the essence of the imminent (any moment) return of the Lord Jesus. The disciples were told in Acts 1:11 that this same Jesus would return in like manner as he left. They were however not told when. The same is true when Jesus spoke to his disciples in St. John 14:2-3.

He declared he would come and receive them unto himself. He did not say when. The early church therefore maintained a spirit of expectancy. See James 5:8; Titus 2:13. That mind set was the order of the day in the early church, to the extent that they believed that Jesus would have literally returned in their own lifetime. It is important to note that, the rapture being imminent, causes God's people to live and to lead holy lives.

> 1 John 3:3, *"he that hath this hope in Him (the return of Jesus) purifies himself even as He is pure"*.

Now let us return to the Jewish marriage ceremony which was mentioned earlier. We want to make the point that the rapture is symbolic of a Jewish wedding or marriage ceremony. In this ceremony there is a concept called **home taking** and occurs when the prospective groom would secretly come for the expected bride. One of his groomsmen would give a cry, "the bridegroom cometh" and that triggers a series of activities. Paul later made it clear that he espoused us to one Christ, *"For I am jealous over*

you with Godly jealousy: for I have espoused you to one husband ...." 2 Cor. 11:2.

Again, a Jewish wedding ceremony term. Espoused is what we would call in our western culture, 'engaged'. In Eph. 5:25-32, Paul again links the Church (the bride of Christ) with a marital relationship. This linkage is sealed with Rev. 19:7-9,

> *"Let us be glad and rejoice, and give honour to him: for the marriage of the Lamb is come, and his wife hath made herself ready. And to her was granted that she should be arrayed in fine linen, clean and white: for the fine linen is the righteousness of saints. And he saith unto me, Write, Blessed are they which are called unto the marriage supper of the Lamb. And he saith unto me, These are the true sayings of God".*

The logical question that is to be expected then is "How does this all tie together with the Rapture?" Let us explore from the beginning.

The wedding event begins with the groom to be establishing a marriage covenant with his bride to be. In so doing, he becomes espoused to her. To reach to this stage, the groom would have left his father's house and visited the house of the prospective bride (and her parents), and arrange the covenant price, which is called the dowry. Once the dowry is paid, the groom would then leave the house of the bride, go back to his father's house, usually for a period of one year, and during this time prepare (build) the house that would then be the future matrimonial home.

Let us look at the correlation here.

Jesus left the Father's house above and came to earth to be espoused to his bride (the Church) 2 Cor. 11:2. To reach to the point of the espousal, and have the covenant established, there had to be a purchase price or dowry, as any Jewish young man would have to arrange. The price (dowry) that Jesus paid was the shedding of His life's blood, 1 Cor. 6:20. In so doing, He established the marriage covenant.

The steps after this is that the groom would leave to go back to his father's house and there start preparing a place for his bride, so that later on, he can go for her and bring her back to this place where he prepared. Note Jesus' words, "*…..I go to prepare a place for you, and if I go and prepare a place for you, I will come again and receive you unto myself, that where I am there ye may be also*" John 14:3.

In these ancient Israeli wedding ceremonies, the bride did not know the exact day that the groom to be would return for her. She would have a fair idea of the period however, and so would have been preparing throughout the period and more-so as the "period" approached. In fact, the exact date was something that only the groom's father knew. This amazingly reflects Jesus' words in relation to the matter of his return, where he said, "***But of that day and hour no one knows, not even the angels in heaven, nor the son, but only the father***", Mark 13:32.

The final stage of the ceremony is when the groom returns for the bride. Before he reaches her home, one of his groomsmen would have gone ahead, and near the bride's house would shout with excitement,

"The bridegroom is coming"!

The bride, knowing he would have been coming, but not knowing exactly which night, would quickly refresh herself, get her maids together, and march out to meet him along the way. The groom never actually goes up to her home and knocks on her door. She always goes out and meets him along the way.

At this point, the bride enters into a box-like carriage that has handles (called the Aperion). In Hebrew, the word is "nisuim" and it means "to lift up" or "to carry". She would enter the carriage and be lifted by the men who then carried her to meet the groom. This is exactly what happens in the Rapture. When Jesus comes for the Church, He is not coming down to where we are living now (earth), but we are going to meet him part way, just like in this ceremony.

He comes in the air, and we will hear the shout and will actually go (rise) "lift up"/"be carried" to meet

Him. I am sure that by now you see where we are going, *"For the Lord Himself shall descend from heaven with a shout…. then we which are alive and remain shall be caught up together with them in the clouds, to meet the Lord in the air …..*" 1 Thess. 4:16-17.

Finally, the groom would take the bride back to his father's house, where a place (matrimonial home) would have been prepared. Now recall Jesus' words, *"…..I go to prepare a place for you……. I will come again and receive you unto myself……*" John 14:3.

Now, when that Jewish couple got to the house that the groom prepared, they are locked away for a period of time, usually seven days. This process of taking the bride to the new home is called the "hometaking" – as was outlined earlier. They call this place the bridal chamber - the 'Huppah' as the Jews called it. The original term literally meant "room" or "covering" or "chamber". It was specially built for the bride and groom at the father's home. See Psalm 19:5 and Joel 2:15 where it is mentioned. It is here that they consummated the relationship that they covenanted into at the start. Note, they go into the chamber and is hidden away for a set period. Isaiah 26:20, *"Come, my people, enter thou into thy chambers, and shut thy doors about thee: hide thyself as it were for a little moment, until the indignation be overpast"*.

At the end of that seven days period (a period of seven), the groom would come out with his bride and present her officially for the first time for all to see. This exactly mirrors what happens at and after the Rapture. At the Rapture we are taken up to heaven, and as such will be missing from earth. This is like the locking away by the bride and groom in the Jewish wedding. We will be taken to our matrimonial home (in heaven) and be in the bridal chamber for seven years (a period of seven).

During this time on earth it will be the tribulation period. However, the Church (the bride), will not be there. We will be locked away in the bridal chamber until the wrath passes over. Just as was described in Isaiah 26.

At the end of the seven years tribulation, the Lord will come back to earth, this time **with** His Church (bride) and will show her as such to the world; and thereafter establish the millennial kingdom. Notice the Jewish wedding term that Isaiah used – "***come into thy chamber and shut thy door***". That is exactly what we discussed earlier, where at a point in the ceremony, they come together and are locked away for a seven-day period. This locking away is called in Hebrew, 'Hu' meaning "the chamber". There they are undisturbed, irrespective of all activities outside. This imagery is clear and unmistakable.

We see from this then where the groom first appears for the bride and then some time after he appears with his bride to present her for all to see her. We see the application of this where he first comes for his bride at the meeting in the air (the Rapture) and then afterwards Jesus Christ comes back with his bride on the earth (the second coming). In the Rapture, He does not come with power and the angels, with all eyes beholding Him.

He comes in the air for His people and takes them back to heaven with Him. This to consummate the marriage ceremony as we just discussed in Revelations. He comes back to earth however, sometime after with his Church and this is the point where every eye shall see him, Rev. 19:11-12; Jude 14. This is the second coming or the revelation. We describe this as one coming in two stages:

    First stage   - The Rapture

    Second stage - The Revelation of Jesus Christ

The Rapture brings joy to the heart of all those who accept Jesus Christ as Lord and Saviour. It is important to make the point here that the Rapture is only for those that are saved. It does not matter how often one attends church or gives to the church. Or how good one treats their neighbour. To be in the Rapture you must be born again.

The table below gives an overview of the distinction between the Rapture and the Second Coming of Jesus Christ:

The Rapture	The Second Coming of Jesus Christ
Jesus comes **for** His saints (1 Thess. 4:14-16)	Jesus comes **with** His saints (Rev. 19:11-12; Jude 14)
Jesus comes in the clouds (1 Thess. 4:17)	Jesus comes to the earth (Zech. 14:4-5)
The rapture is secret and swift (1 Cor 15:50-54)	The second coming is visible to all (Rev. 1:7; Matt. 24:29-30)
The rapture is imminent (takes place at any moment 1 Thess. 2:13; 1 Thess. 4:14-17)	The second coming will occur after the other end time events take place (Matt. 24:15-30
Christ takes the church to heaven St. John 14:13	Christ brings the saints to earth. Rev.19: 14; Zech. 14: 4 – 5

The Lord has always been faithful to His people and while He allows us to be tested and tried severely, and even suffer death, as our brothers and sisters in the early church, the Lord never pours out his wrath on the righteous.

I make this point here because some do believe that the Lord will not rapture the Church before the tribulation. Their argument is, why would God cause all the members of the Church today to escape the tribulation, when those in the early church had to endure? I make the point that Christians in every age go through persecutions or some other hardships in some form or shape. God rapturing us before the tribulation is not to shield us from hardships or difficult times. He knows we have been enduring and fighting on just like the saints of old. He delivers us because this period represents the point where God is going to pour out his wrath upon Israel for their rejection of the Messiah, and also upon Gentile peoples for the degrading place where they all have now come.

This act by God to remove or separate His people from his judgment, and the pouring of his wrath, is consistent with the way that he always operated. Now the book of Revelation in Chapter 6 and verse 17 tells us "...*the great day of his wrath is come; and who shall be able to stand?*" Look also at Revelation 16:1, "*And I heard a great voice out of the temple saying to the seven angels, Go your ways, and pour out the vials of the wrath of God upon the earth*".

We have already said that God never pours his wrath upon the righteous. We therefore are confident the scriptures show us a pattern in the way that God deals with the righteous when he is to pour out his wrath. In Genesis when God was about to pour out his judgement on the earth because of the wickedness of mankind, Enoch was translated before the judgement. Noah, another righteous man was sheltered in an ark throughout the judgement. See Genesis 5:21-24 and Genesis 6:13.

Again, God had enough with Sodom and Gomorrah and his judgment was about to be poured out on the city to destroy it. Note however that Lot, a righteous man, was in the city and as long as Lot was there, God refused to destroy Sodom. When Lot came out, God's judgement only then was poured out, Genesis 19:15-22; 2 Peter 2:6-9. Then finally we wish to use the harlot Rahab to cement this point. She was a Gentile and was saved from the destruction of Jericho when it was being destroyed. Rahab the harlot, was a type of the Gentile believer, who although is unworthy, is saved by the grace of God by way of the rapture and before the judgement of God falls. (Note Joshua 2:1, 12-14 and Jeremiah 6:22-25).

> Isaiah 26:19-21, "*Thy dead men shall live, together with my dead body shall they arise. Awake and sing, ye that dwell in the dust: for thy dew is as the dew of herbs, and the earth shall cast out the dead. Come, my people, enter thou into thy chambers, and shut thy doors about thee: hide thyself as it were for a little moment, until the indignation be overpast. For behold, the Lord cometh out of this place to punish the inhabitants of the earth for their iniquity: the earth also shall disclose her blood, and shall no more cover the slain*".

We see in Rev. 3:10, "*will be kept __from__ the great time of temptation and trial on the earth*". The word *'from'* here is the Greek word *'ek'* which means *'exit out of'* or *'separation from'*. Notice Jesus' words to the disciples in Philadelphia. He said He would keep them *'from'* the hour of temptation..., not keep them 'through it'. It is important to note that in Chapters 1-3 of Revelation, the Church is mentioned 19 times and the Church was right here on earth.

In Revelation 4 through 19, which covers the entire tribulation period, there is no mention of the Church at all on earth. What could have happened from Revelation 4 that accounts for this glaring absence? Let us look at Rev. 4:1, where the Apostle John heard a voice which said, **"Come up hither"**. He then stood before the presence of God and saw 24 elders with crowns on their heads. If we examine scriptures like 2 Tim. 4:8,

> *"henceforth there is laid up for me a crown of righteousness, which the Lord, the righteous judge, shall give me at that day: and not to me only, but unto all them that love his appearing",*

We see that these elders all had their crowns.

We accept that the 24 elders are a representation of the Church – Revelation 5:4; when John saw them, they were already in heaven, for they already had their crowns, and these crowns, as we have learned, are issued at the Judgement Seat of Christ (Bema) – 2 Corinthians 5:10.

So, John would have been taken up to heaven in his vision at a time after the Rapture and saw the saints already in receipt of their crown (the Rapture would therefore have taken place). It was after this scene in heaven that he then saw the events of the tribulation taking place on earth, and through this entire period no mention is made of the Church on earth. Furthermore, the Bible makes it clear that the Church will be gone before the lawless one, the Antichrist is manifested on the scene 2 Thess. 2:1-9.

Church of God, this great event is imminent. I believe that very soon the archangel will blow the trumpet and the dead in Christ will rise. Those still alive will be changed instantaneously and rise also to meet Jesus in the air. Oh! What a day that will be!

CHAPTER 7

ARMAGEDDON

The word 'Armageddon' drives fear in the hearts and minds of many, even when they do not understand fully the meaning of the word. It is associated with war, devastation, and destruction. It is used by many as they envisage a scenario of a blood bath and total devastation and annihilation. When the Japanese attacked Pearl Harbour in 1941, this pulled America into World War 2. While the war was progressing, there was a top-secret mission that was being undertaken by the United States of America called the 'Manhattan Project'. They were developing the Atomic Bomb. This weapon of mass destruction was to be used on two occasions in Japan.

On August 6, 1945, the Americans dropped the first atomic bomb in Hiroshima in Japan. Two days later, they dropped the second in the city of Nagasaki. Mankind has never seen this nightmare. The world was dumbstruck, and a new era never before seen dawned on mankind. After the dropping of the bomb, the fiery inferno that ensued, and the ultimate surrender of Japan, the US war general, Douglas McArthur made a very profound statement. He said, "A new era is upon us ... we have had our last chance. If we do not now devise some greater and more equitable system, Armageddon will be at our door".

Since that time there has been unease amongst men as somewhere in their subconscious, there is that nagging consciousness of what can happen to mankind given the new atomic age and the ambition of men to rule the world. What then is Armageddon and why does the term invoke so much fear and dread? Does the possibility of a blood bath in still fear in our future? Does the Bible have anything to say about this?

The name Armageddon occurs once in the scriptures and is indeed used in a setting that is very chilling. Let us read Revelation 16:12-16,

> *"And the sixth angel poured out his vial upon the great river Euphrates; and the water thereof was dried up, that the way of the kings of the east might be prepared. And I saw three unclean spirits like frogs come out of the mouth of the dragon, and out of the mouth of the beast, and out the mouth of the false prophet. For they are the spirits of devils, working miracles, which go forth unto the kings of the earth and of the whole world, to gather them to the battle of that great day of God Almighty. Behold, I come as a thief. Blessed is he that watcheth, and keepeth his garments, lest he walk naked, and they see his shame. And he gathered them together into a place called in the Hebrew tongue Armageddon".*

So, where is the place called Armageddon? The Greek form of the word – Armageddon is the one most accepted. At the root of this Greek form are two Hebrew words, 'Har and Megiddo'. 'Har' is a regular Hebrew term appearing in scriptures (Exodus 3:1; Genesis 7:20). It means mountain. 'Megiddo' is the name of a city in ancient Israel at the base of the Carmel Ridge. This city is also mentioned in scriptures (1 Kings 4:12; Judges 5:19; Joshua 12:21), where people were slayed in wars. Thus, the root word suggests the mount of slaughter. It appears that Armageddon was a major battlefield of this region.

Megiddo stood on the edge of the plain of the valley of Jezreel. This valley is mentioned in the Bible. Many significant battles in the life of Israel took place here. The Bible tells us of a conflict between Israel and the Canaanites at this location. The Israelites were victorious, with the help of God of course, and what a celebration they had. Listen to the songs of victory that they belted out and how it indicated what God did for them by the waters of Megiddo:

> *"The Kings came, they fought; then fought the Kings of Canaan; At Tanakh, by the waters of Megiddo; they got no spoils of silver. From heaven fought the stars, from their courses they fought against Sisera. The torrent Kishon swept them away, the onrushing torrent, the torrent Kishon. March on, my soul with might"* - Judges 5:19-21.

Similarly, the battle between Israel (under the leadership of Gideon) and the Midianites took place at this same location, and again Israel prevailed miraculously by the hand of Almighty God. With only 300 men, Israel took on the mighty Midianites and routed them. Notice the two formidable foes (the Canaanites and the Midianites), that came against Israel at the 'Valley of Megiddo', and were soundly beaten.

In both cases God intervened and ensured victory for Israel. It appears as if for His own reasons, God pulled these armies to take on Israel at this particular location, and then demolished them by His mighty power. It is as if this is the place where God has reserved to destroy Israel's arch enemies. It is at this very location that God will mobilise the armies of the world for the battle of Armageddon.

Hundreds of years ago, Joel the prophet of God prophesied in Chapter 3:9-14,

> *"Proclaim ye this among the Gentiles; Prepare war, wake up the mighty men, let all the men of war draw near; let them come up. Beat your plow shares into swords, and your pruning hooks into spears: let the weak say I am strong (I am a warrior). Assemble yourselves, and come, all ye heathen and gather yourselves together round about: thither cause thy mighty ones to come down, O Lord. Let the heathen be wakened and*

come up to the valley of Jehoshaphat; for there will I sit to judge all the heathen round about. Put ye in the sickle, for the harvest is ripe: come, get you down; for the press is full, the vats overflow; for their wickedness is great. Multitudes, multitudes in the valley of decision: for the day of the Lord is near in the valley of decision".

Just as we saw with the Canaanites and the Midianites, God will cause the armies of the enemies of Israel to gather at Armageddon. Their plans are to destroy the holy city and the people of God. This will unleash the final reign of terror on God's people. As it approaches the time of the end, another series of world activity will emerge that will present a certain geopolitical atmosphere that ultimately leads to Armageddon.

Prior to 1948, not much emphasis was placed on the Middle East, except as it relates to Arab oil. The dominant superpower in the region was the United States of America. The USSR, which was the other superpower, was nowhere active as the U.S. in the region. The Bible in Ezekiel 38 made some startling predictions about Israel being invaded by a nation to their north. If we run a straight line from Jerusalem, direct north, it runs straight into Moscow. This is the capital of Russia.

"Son of man, set thy face against Gog, the land of Magog, the chief prince of

> *Meshech and Tubal, and prophecy against him. And say, thus saith the Lord God; Behold, I am against thee, O Gog, the chief prince of Meschech and Tubal: and I will turn thee back, and put locks in thy jaws, and I will bring forth, and all thy army, horses and horsemen, all of them clothed with all sorts of armour, even a great company with bucklers and shield, all of them handling swords: Persia, Ethiopia, and Libya with them: all of them with shield and helmet; Gomer' and all his bands: the house of Togarmah of the north quarters, and all his bands: and many people with thee".*
> *Ezekiel. 38: 2-6.*

Recall that prior to 1948, there was no nation called Israel. For nearly two thousand years, this people were dispersed across other nations and had no homeland. When prophecy students spoke about Israel being invaded by Russia and others, they were ridiculed as there were no nation of Israel- at the time. Just to highlight how clear the prophecy is. It spoke about Russia invading Israel with a contingent of other forces.

This proves the validity of the word of prophecy. If Israel was not there, it had to re-emerge. That it did in 1948 when the nation of Israel was reborn. The prophecy still stands.

Now that the nation of Israel is a recognized state of the nations of the world, the Middle East has been transformed into a different region. It has become a literal melting pot where Israel and their Arab and Persian neighbours are perpetually at war. In fact, since 1948 when Israel became a nation, they have been engaged in wars as follows:

- 1948 – War of Independence
- 1956 – Suez War
- 1967 – The Six Day war
- 1973 – The Yum Kippur War
- 1987 – 1993 – Intifada
- 2000 – Second Intifada
- 2006 – Israel/Lebanon War

The point being made here is that all of Israel's neighbours are uncomfortable with them existing as a nation and from 1948 (when the nation was re-established) there has been a constant push to get consensus and to build Arab support to surround Israel and choke them off. This passion will reach its peak during the tribulation period, and as it approaches the ending of this period, the desire will be at fever pitch and Russia will make a move against Israel. Although the battle itself will occur towards the end of the tribulation, we are witnessing the geopolitical alignments taking place today.

Critics scoffed at the idea of Russia attacking the nation of Israel today for two main reasons:

1. The distance of Russia away from Israel for them to move military personnel and hardware with Israel being so alert and generally prepared. By the time there is a formidable build up, these Russians would have been under pressure from the Israeli Defence Force.

2. The fact that the United States has such a long-and well-established presence in this region. Recall that the U.S. is a staunch supporter of Israel and is the arch enemy of Russia. A strong U.S. presence there as a military superpower would be a great disincentive for Russia to even contemplate invading.

Notice today the changing tide of the region. A completely new U.S. policy with respect to their armed forces have resulted in the withdrawal of massive amount of U.S. troops from the region that literally created a vacuum in the region. This happened at a time when ISIS was on the verge of toppling the Government of Syria. With the U.S. pulling troops from the region and Syria, a well-established country in the Middle East on the brink of collapse, the unthinkable happened. Russia filled the vacuum. They came in under the egis of assisting the Government of Syria and stopping their collapse.

Now for the first time in history, Russia has a solid footing in the Middle East and their troops are based in Syria, who shares common border with Israel.

This is unthinkable. Yet it is reality. Russia is now in Israel's backyard. A few months ago, this would have been unheard of. According to the scriptures, Russia will plan and establish a coalition with surrounding nations.

Who are these coalition partners? The prophet Ezekiel identifies them. Ezekiel 38:5-6:

- Persia – this is Iran
- Cush – this is Ethiopia/Sudan
- Phut – this is Libya
- Gomer - Germany
- Togarmah – Turkey

Note that these are predominantly Muslim countries totally opposed to the existence of the nation of Israel. The question that begs to be asked is, "Why do we think this represents a period yet future, and then lead up to the battle of Armageddon"? Two very important facts come out at us immediately when we consider this question? One is that as was stated earlier, Israel would have to be back in their homeland again.

> *"After many days thou shalt be visited: in the latter years thou shalt come into the land that is brought back from the sword, and is gathered out of many people, against mountains of Israel, which have been always waste: but it is brought forth out of the nations, and they shall*

dwell safely all of the them". Ezekiel 38:8.

The other is that it will happen when Israel is in the land and experiencing a time of peace and safety.

> *"And thou shalt say, I will go up to the land of unwalled villages; and I will go to them that be at rest, that dwell safely, all of them dwelling without walls, and having neither bars nor gates"- Ezekiel 38:11.*

Israel's experience since they became a nation does not reflect any period of peace, tranquillity, and safety. We have seen that by the many wars they have fought since becoming a nation. It is worse now in 2020 than any time before. The only period of peace and safety for Israel is coming in the future when the Antichrist is revealed and establishes a peace treaty with Israel. This treaty literally guarantees their safety and security in their homeland. This gives them a sense of freedom they never experienced before and so they are free to re-engage in their temple sacrifice and way of worship.

Somehow, as a result of the peace accord and their resumption of temple activities, they will be lulled into a false sense of security and evidently will be taken off guard when the invading armies strike. It appears that the campaign of Armageddon will be kick-started here, and God will intervene to destroy the Russian forces – and those that came up with him Eze. 38:18-22).

This is not the end, however. Other nations will join in because this entire saga will without doubt escalate into an all-out world war. The campaign of Armageddon reaches its crescendo when the armies of the nations are gathered in that middle eastern region. Revelation 16:6, *"And he gathered them together into a place called in Hebrew tongue Armageddon"*. This will be the supposed fatal blow. Satan's final attempt to destroy the nation of Israel. Some are out there out of shear hatred for the Jewish people. The heights of anti- Semitism. Others are there out of greed and red eye, attempting to capture the great natural resources of the region to achieve and maintain superpower status. Yet others will be there simply because they were ordered to be there.

Though Israel is the common target, the major armies also have their own separate agendas. At least two major armies are called out based on the following passage:

> Revelation 16: 12-14, *"And the sixth angel poured out the vial upon the great river Euphrates, and the water thereof was dried up, that the way of the kings of the east might prepared. And I saw three unclean spirits like frogs come out of the mouth of the dragon and out of the mouth of the beast, and out of the mouth of the false prophet. For they are the*

> *spirits of devils, working miracles, which go forth unto the kings of the earth and the whole world, to gather them to the battle of the that great day of God Almighty".*

One is the king of the east, amassing an army of 200 million soldiers. Practically all accept this to be China, the rising superpower of the east. China has become a formidable economic and military power and continue their rise and expansion. The other is the Antichrist with the armies from the rest of the world that he will have control over. The conflict would have begun, and a massive display of the military power demonstrated. Amid this fighting and mayhem, a sound comes from another direction – another army joins the war. It is none other than the Lord Jesus Christ and His army (the Church of Jesus Christ) coming out of heaven itself.

The armies in conflict recognizing something major happening, that is unprecedented and unexplainable, join their military forces to unite against the invading army. Rev. 19:19, *"And I saw the beast, and the kings of the earth and their armies, gather to make war against him that sat on the horse, and against his army"*. Jesus and the armies of heaven thoroughly rout the Antichrist and all the armies that were engaged in this battle. It will be a very serious affair as the armies of the nation amass over in the Middle East to take on the nation of Israel, with a view to totally annihilate them.

This battle represents Satan's attempt again to wipe out the Jewish people once and for all. Especially in recent years, the leaders of Iran and others of their neighbours have vowed to push them into the sea. The headlines in the newspapers across the region are calling for and supporting the pushing of Israel into the sea. There is a hatred for the nation of Israel that is beyond comprehension.

Clearly Satan knows it is through Israel that all the nations of the earth will be blessed, Genesis 22:18 – *"And in thy seed shall all the nations of the earth be blessed"*. Messiah, the Prince, came out of Israel and because of Him, salvation came to mankind. Through this same Prince, Jesus Christ, God will rule over the people of Israel as he had always wanted to do from Old Testament times and will indeed rule over the earth in the Millennium. Satan definitely wants to crush this people in his attempt to stop this from happening, and so he deceives the leaders of the nations and propels them to advance on Israel with a view to exterminate them.

Nevertheless, the Lord is fully in charge and His will is going to be accomplished. (*"I will gather all nations against Jerusalem to battle"* Zechariah 14:2). Listed below are some of the names given to Armageddon as described in scriptures:

- Valley of decision – Joel 3:13-14
- Day of vengeance of our God – Isaiah 61:1-2

- Great winepress of the wrath of God - Revelation 14:19; 19:15
- The battle of the great day of God Almighty – Revelation 16:14
- The supper of the Great God – Revelation 19:17

How the battle is described makes it abundantly clear that it will be brutal. In addition to the above description, blood will flow to the horses' bridle, for a distance of 180 miles – Revelation 14:20. Revelation gives a chilling account of the angel of God calling the fowls of the air to come to eat of the flesh of dead men.

Notice, <u>all</u> the fowls of the air are called, signalling that there will be a massive amount of corpse by virtue of the fierceness of the battle. Revelation 19:17 – 18,

> *"And I saw an angel standing in the sun; and he cried with a loud voice, saying to all the fowls that fly in the midst of heaven, Come and gather yourselves together unto the supper of the great God; that ye may eat the flesh of kings, and the flesh of captains, and the flesh of mighty men, and the flesh of horses, and of them that sit on them, and the **flesh of all men**, both free and bond, both small and great".*

Horrific! This represents the end of the battle. The Lord Jesus and the armies of heaven that came with Him ultimately bring the campaign at Armageddon to a close by defeating the armies of earth and taking authority over earth itself.

It is after this moment that He moves to establish the Millennial Kingdom right here on earth, ushering in the one thousand years of peace, administering justly.

CHAPTER 8

GETTING READY OR READY WAITING?

The Horsemen are riding, the system facilitating the Mark of the Beast has emerged, the New World Order is upon us, and things that people would generally brush aside as ridiculous and sensational are now being seriously pondered. The thought that things now emerging synchronise so closely with what was spoken of in such details and clarity in scriptures, is staggering.

Many are now taking a second look at a book they once scorned, or even feared—The Bible. The question being asked is, "Can the Bible really be true"? The answer is a resounding Yes!

A close examination of scriptural prophecies shows fulfilment at a rate that is staggering to the human mind. We are not talking about 80% or 90% accuracy. We are speaking about scores of predictions of events that have been fulfilled to the last word—100%. These fulfilments have been verified and authenticated in many instances by people (archaeologists and historians) who are unbelievers! This then represents compelling evidence that the Bible is divinely inspired and must therefore be taken seriously. If the predictions that were made in the Old Testament came through, which they did, then we can be sure that those presented in the earlier pages of this book will come through in a **similar** manner!

To cement the point being made, let us consider a few of these predictions and their actual fulfilment.

PROPHECIES	FULFILLMENT
Jesus would be born in Bethlehem – Micah 5:2	*"Now when Jesus was born in Bethlehem of Judea, in the day of Herod the king ....."* – St. Matt. 2:1
He would be betrayed for thirty (30) pieces of silver – Zechariah 11:2	*"....what will ye give me and I will deliver him unto you? And they covenanted with him for thirty (30) pieces of silver"* – Matt. 26:15
His hand and his feet to be pierced – Psalm 22:16	*"And when they were come to the place, which is called Calvary, there they crucified him,..."* St. Luke 23:33
He was beaten, spat upon, boxed. Isaiah 50:6	*"Then did they spit in his face and buffeted him: and others smote him with the palm of their hands"* - Matt. 26:67
Jesus would enter Jerusalem on a colt – Zechariah 9:9	*"And they brought him to Jesus: and they cast their garments upon the colt, and they set Jesus thereon... the disciples began to rejoice and praise God...."* – Luke 19:35-35

The prophecies and their fulfilment noted above speak for themselves. The point being reinforced here is that if the Bible was so accurate in relation to these predictions surrounding Christ's first coming, then we can be sure that they will be equally accurate about the events surrounding His second coming.

In all, there are approximately 331 prophecies fulfilled by Jesus, from the Old Testament to the New Testament. Events and details that could not be close to coincidental!

If the things outlined in this volume are true, and they most assuredly are, there should be an air of greater urgency and seriousness in the way we conduct ourselves as children of God, and the way in which we undertake kingdom business. The Apostle Peter outlined it appropriately in 2 Peter 3:11,

> ***"Seeing then that all these things shall be dissolved, what manner of persons ought ye to be in all holy conversation and godliness".***

This admonition by the Apostle Peter is consistent with the way in which Jesus Himself advised the disciples to conduct themselves in daily living, knowing the end time events and the end of the world reality. We must not lose sight of a very important element of Jesus' Olivet discourse.

Immediately after discussing things about the signs of his second coming and the end of the world in Matt. 24:29-31,

> *"But immediately after the tribulation of those days the sun will be darkened, and the moon will not give its light, and the stars will fall from the sky, and the powers of the heavens will be shaken. And then the sign of the Son of Man will appear in the sky, and then all the tribes of the earth will mourn, and they will see the Son of Man coming on the clouds of the sky with power and great glory. And He will send forth his angels with a great trumpet and they will gather together His elect from the four winds, from one end of the sky to the other".*

Jesus goes seamlessly into Matthew 25, where he enumerated three parables, all of which relate to our living and our responsibility even as we await his coming and the end of the world system as we know it.

Firstly, he related the parable of the ten virgins – Matt. 25:1-13. We know the story well and we appreciate that all were virgins, all had lamps, but not all were properly prepared for the coming of the bride groom. Preparation requires planning, introspection and constant assessment of our lives according to the requirements of the word of God. By the time they moved to be fully prepared for the bridegroom he came and moved on. Although they knew he was coming, they were not ready when he did! What a tragedy it will be should we have all the information about the end times, know the season that we are in, be fully persuaded of his return, and then miss the Rapture! Jesus' admonition in this parable was simply this, "keep watch, because you do not know the day nor the hour"

Secondly, he related the parable of the talents – Matthew 25:14-30,

> *"For it is just like a man about to go on a journey, who called his own servants and entrusted his possession to them. To one he gave five talents, to another, two and to another, one, each according to his own ability; and he went on his journey. Immediately the one who had received the five talents went and traded with them and gained five more talents. In the same manner the one who had received two talents gained two more. But he who received the one talent went away and dug a hole in the ground and hid his master's money. Now after a long time the master of those servants came and settled accounts with them. The one who had received the five talents came up and brought five more talents, saying "Master, you entrusted five talents to me. See, I have gained five more talents," His master said to him, "Well done, good and faithful servant. You were faithful*

with a few things, I will put you in charge of many things; enter into the joy of your master". Also, the one who had received the two talents came up and said, "Master, you entrusted two talents to me. See, I have gained two more talents". His master said to him, "Well done, good and faithful servant. You were faithful with a few things I will put you in charge of many things; enter into the joy of your master". And the one also who had received the one talent came up and said, "Master, I knew you were hard man, reaping where you did not sow and gathering where you scattered no seed. And I was afraid and went away and hid your talent in the ground. See, you have what is yours". But his master answered and said to him, "You wicked, lazy servant, you knew that I reap where I did not sow and gathered where I scattered no seed. Then you ought to have put my money in the bank, and on my arrival, I would have received my money back with interest.

Therefore, take away the talent from him, and give it to the one who has ten talents".

For to everyone who has, more shall be given, and he will have an abundance; but from the one who does not have, even what he does have shall be taken away.

> ***Throw out the worthless servant into outer darkness; in that place there will be weeping and gnashing of teeth".***

Again, this is a well-known parable where a man travelled on a far journey and entrusted his belongings to his workers. Clearly, he was away for an extended period; to the extent that his workers moved to invest properly what he advanced them before he went on his journey. The story related that there were three of them and all three received talents. Two of them invested their talents and made their returns which they presented to their boss upon his return. The other had wasted his time, was slothful, negligent and evidently undisciplined. He did not generate any returns for his boss. He faced him empty handed upon his return. What is the lesson here? We know the signs are indicating that Jesus is coming. When he left, he bestowed responsibilities on us as believers. He expects us to be good stewards/managers of what we are doing for him, so that when he returns and asks us to give an account of our stewardship, we can with joy show how we multiplied the talents he gave us.

Where is the wisdom then in knowing that He is coming again and understanding that we will be requested to give an account, and when he actually comes, we stand before him with nothing to declare?

Let us be determined that what we have gleaned from this book will be used to inspire us to work for our Master, because His coming is near, and when he does come, there will be a period of recounting how we managed what He has bestowed us. Let us be ready!

Finally, he related the parable of the sheep and the goats. This parable references a time when the Lord returns to separate those who faithfully served Him from those who did not.

It must be abundantly clear by now that all three of these parables emanate from his discourse about the end times. The first is that the bridegroom returned (end-time), the second is that the owner of the place left on a far journey and then returned (end-time), and the third parable relates to the time of the judgement when Jesus returns to separate the sheep from the goats (end-time).

Jesus related these parables to stir our consciousness to the fact that even as we look around and see the signs of His coming and therefore await His coming, we have a responsibility to properly and faithfully occupy until He comes.

Yet another parable was spoken about the faithful and unfaithful servants (St. Matthew 24:45-51).

> *Who then is a faithful and wise servant, whom his lord hath made ruler over his household, to give them meat in due season? Blessed is that servant, whom his lord when he cometh shall find so doing.*

> *Verily I say unto you, That he shall make him ruler over all his goods. But and if that evil servant shall say in his heart, My lord delayeth his coming; And shall begin to smite his fellow servants, and to eat and drink with the drunken; The lord of that servant shall come in a day when he looketh not for him, and in an hour that he is not aware of, And shall cut him asunder, and appoint him his portion with the hypocrites: there shall be weeping and gnashing of teeth.*

The parable has to do with how we treat people even as we await the return of the Master.

The Lord will use as part of his measuring stick, the way we treated the hungry, the thirsty, the homeless, the naked, the sick and the prisoners, in executing his judgement.

So as we garner information about end times and seek to understand the sequence of events and all that is associated with Jesus' return; let us seek to also understand our responsibility as we wait, so we can be ready, to be watching and to be working in the Kingdom!

Although the parables highlighted in the preceding treatise assume (not necessarily by design) that the stewards are in the kingdom, i.e. are saved, part of the "Getting Ready [in order to be] Ready Waiting" process is accepting Salvation—being saved. I would just like to take a moment to share on the important life decision of accepting the salvation of God. Let me begin with a well-known scripture:

> *For God so loved the world that He gave His only begotten Son, that whosoever believeth in Him shall not perish, but have everlasting life.* St. John 3:16

Jesus came to earth to reconcile sinful man to a holy God. He accomplished this through His death on the cross, where His shed blood atoned for the sins of mankind. Not only did He die and was buried, but He rose again to give us eternal hope.

As pointed out in preceding chapters, we are at a crucial point in the annals of human history. Something major is about to happen. Many have testified that they literally feel it in the air, and as such are asking what to do in order to be ready for what is to come. The individual who is unsaved, but who is aware that he is in need of God, must submit to God's WORD regarding salvation. The Bible clearly states that *"all have sinned, and come short of the glory of God"* (Romans 3:23). There is absolutely none righteous. Remaining in this state of unrighteousness makes one a candidate for hell. Praise God, however, for his love and grace, which moved him to prepare a way of escape for the lost.

A very important note here: There are some who totally reject the teachings of the Bible concerning a literal hell. They argue that there is absolutely no way that a loving and gracious Saviour would condemn man whom He made, to such a terrible place. The WORD of God is very clear on the matter, however. Revelation 20:12-15 makes it clear that after that great judgement day, death and hell shall be cast into the lake of fire. It is this same lake of which the scripture declares, *"...their worm diet not."* (St. Mark 9: 43-48) In other words, it is an everlasting state. What then must the unsaved do to ensure that they do not end up in that place? It is mandatory (a must) that you believe in the Lord Jesus Christ. It is the man, Jesus, who did a mighty work to bridge this gap between a holy God and fallen man. By His death on the cross in a place called Calvary. This message is the greatest message of love ever told. The great God of heaven, the Creator of the ends of the earth, took on human nature, and was manifest in the flesh (1 Timothy 3:16), so that He could go all the way to Calvary to ensure salvation for all mankind. This event is as real as the ground upon which we stand. To believe in the Lord then, is to wholeheartedly accept this fact that Jesus Christ died to save sinners, and to recognise that he did it for **you.**

Having exercised your faith in Jesus in this way, it is important that you now demonstrate this faith by obeying God's simple plan of salvation and **accept the Lord Jesus Christ (Acts 2:38).**

Therefore, to those who are unsaved, it is important that you get salvation now, so that you can be ready and waiting for the Lord's coming. Those of us who are already in the church must ensure that our lamps are trimmed, that is, we are living dedicated and holy lives. There are some simple things that we must do, and if we do them, we will be kept humble and will be prepared for the coming of the Lord. We should spend **much** time in prayer. **Give to God first.** Consistent prayer, fasting and the reading the Word of God is extremely important.

The end of the age is at hand. The horsemen are geared up. The One World system is in place. The pillars of earth as we know it are shaking. The rapture can be any moment now. The end is now here! Let us escape the wrath to come and accept today God's wonderful plan of salvation—a simple prescription that guarantees eternal life. Let us look up, our redemption draweth nigh. Behold He cometh! One Minute to Midnight. The curtains are closing on planet earth.

CHAPTER 9

QUESTIONS AND ANSWERS

After reading the book up to his point, questions naturally will linger in your mind. In early 2020, I was involved in a prophecy conference in Rochester, New York, and there also, questions arose out of the presentations. These questions represent some of the more frequent ones asked, and I hope the answers given will shed more light.

1. Who is the Antichrist and where will he come from?

The Antichrist is a person who will be empowered by Satan during the tribulation. He will be the embodiment of sin and lawlessness (2 Thessalonian 2:3, 8-9), the most dynamic and charismatic political leader that the world has ever seen (Revelation 17:11-12). A man of great intellect (Daniel 8:23) with many descriptions in scripture for example in Isaiah he is called "the king of Babylon" (Isaiah 14:4), in Daniel he is "the little horn" (Daniel 7:8, 8:9) that will come from the same people who destroyed Jerusalem. Jerusalem was destroyed in 70 A.D. by the Romans (Daniel 9:24-27). The Apostle Paul describes him as "the man of sin" (2 Thessalonians 2:3-8) and lastly John calls him the "beast" (Revelation 13:1) and the Antichrist (1 John 2:18). Whatever he is called, he is coming with one agenda, and that is to lead the world into open rebellion against the Most High God (2 Thessalonians 2:10).

The last Gentile world kingdom, the revived Roman Empire, will be headed by the Antichrist (Daniel 2: 7). It is from his headquarters that he will dominate the world for seven years. He will negotiate a peace treaty for Israel and then proceed to build a worldwide empire, using a reunited Europe as his initial political base. In the latter three and a half years of his reign he will declare himself to be god, and he will launch the greatest persecution of the Jews in history. At the second coming of Jesus Christ, the Antichrist will be seized and thrown into the lake of fire, together with his false prophet. (Read Dan. 11:21; 12:4; Rev.13; 19:11-21).

2. What is the Great Tribulation?

The Great Tribulation is the last week of Daniels' seventy weeks Prophecy. It is a seven-year period of time during which there will be a pouring out of the wrath of God on the wicked. The prophets of old often times refer to the great tribulation as either (1) the day of God vengeance (Isaiah 35:4; 61:2),the day of God's judgement (Romans 2:5; Revelation 14:7) or the day of God's wrath (Revelation 6:16-17; 11:18).It is a period of time where "The proud shall be brought low, and the Lord will shake the earth terribly" (Isaiah 2:12-19). This period will begin at the end of the Church Age and will immediately precede the return of the Lord to reign for a thousand years from Mt. Zion in Jerusalem. (Read

Deuteronomy 4:30-31; Jeremiah 30:7-8; Dan. 12:1; Matthew 24:15-31 and Revelation 6-19).

3. **Are we living in the season of the Lord's return?**

Yes. While we cannot tell the actual date of the Lord's return, we can discern the season (Luke 12:56) and many signs around us point to fact that return of the Lord is nigh even at the door.

Jesus, when addressed the disciples on the Mount of Olives, spoke about the proliferation of wars, famine, pestilence and earthquakes in the last days (Matthew 24: 6-7) and he described all these things as the beginning of sorrows or labour pains. Just as is true with labour pains so it is with the coming of the Lord, because as we come closer to the coming of the Lord these signs mentioned by our Lord will become more frequent and more severe.

The Apostle Paul spoke about the emergence of false teachers and preachers in the last day and they will be so convincing that they will draw men to themselves (Acts 20: 29-30). Apostasy seem to be on the increase as many have departed from the faith giving heed to seducing spirits and doctrines of devils (1 Timothy 4:1-2). Then we can see the sign of moral disintegration all over the world, there is an open surge of pornography, extramarital sex, prevalent homosexuality, drugs, divorce and such like. The moral fibre in our society continues to erode as was written by the apostle Paul as a sign in the last days (2 Timothy 3: 1-4).

Then as we look, we see a weakening of the United States and this is rightly so because the Bible was clear that the superpower in the last days will be the revived Roman Empire headed by the Antichrist (Daniel 2:7).

One of the major signs in the last days, one that we cannot ignore, is the re-establishment of the nation of Israel and the Jewish re-occupation of the city of Jerusalem. The Bible always pictures the Lord's return at a time when the Jews are back in the land of Israel and in possession of the city of Jerusalem. Many prophecies in scripture are reliant upon this fact. The Jews must be in their own land before the beginning of the tribulation period. The same is true in relation to the rebuilding of the temple that will exist during the Great Tribulation (Matthew 24:15-16). Read Zechariah 14:1-9 & Luke 21:24.

4. What prophecies must yet be fulfilled before Jesus returns?

One of the reasons for confusion among believers is that they have not properly distinguished between the rapture and the second coming. As it relates to the rapture of the church, there is no prophecy that needs to be fulfilled before Christ returns, and this is based on the nature of the rapture. The rapture is imminent, meaning "about to happen". So, it would be risky to say that the rapture is going to happen in the next minute, but a more factual statement is that the rapture can happen in the next minute. In St John 14:2-3 Jesus told his disciples that He would come again but He did not state when. The same principle applies in Acts 1:11 where the angel said that Jesus would come again, but like Jesus, he did not say when. The rapture can take place at any time and for this reason we find that the church, even from its early days in the first century were in constant expectation of this event (see Phil 3:20-21, James 5:8, Titus 2:13) and we are constantly urged to be on the alert (Read Matt. 24:42-44; 25:1-13 and Luke 12:35-40).

As it relates to the second coming of Jesus Christ, there are many prophecies that must be fulfilled before Jesus returns to reign over the earth. Events such as the rapture of the saints (1 Thessalonian 4:16-17), the revealing of the Antichrist (2 Thessalonians 2:3–10), and the seven year Great Tribulation (Revelation 6-19), to name a few, will be accomplished before Jesus returns. In summary, the rapture can occur any moment (1 Corinthians 15:52), while there are but a few prophecies left to be fulfilled before the second coming or the revelation of Jesus Christ (Titus 2:13).

5. What is the Rapture, and when will it occur?

The rapture is that glorious event where the dead in Christ will be resurrected, where the living Christians will be translated in their resurrected body and both groups will be caught up to meet Christ in the air and be taken to heaven with Him (John 14: 1-3, 1 Cor 15: 51-54, 1 Thess. 4: 13-17).

The exact timing of the Rapture is not revealed in the Bible, but the Scriptures infer that it will occur right before the Great Tribulation. (Read Luke 21:28, 36; 1 Thess. 1:10 and Rev. 3:10).

6. Will the Church go through the Tribulation?

This is a question that has been on the mind of many for a long time, but as we examine what the scriptures teach, we are more inclined to go with the fact that the church will _not_ go through the tribulation.

As discussed before, the Great Tribulation is the last seven-year period of Daniel's Prophecy of the seventy weeks (Daniel 9:27), where the wrath of God will be poured on the earth (Revelation 16:1). Scriptures clearly teach us that the wrath of God is reserved for God's enemies (Nahum 1:2) and is revealed against the ungodly (Romans 1:18). As it relates to the church of God, God promised to make a way of escape from this time period of trouble. He made a promise to the church that he "will keep them from the hour of temptation, which shall come upon all the world, to try them that dwell upon the earth" - Revelation 3:10. The word "from" used in

Revelation 3:10 is from the Greek preposition *"ek"* and it carries the idea of being "separated from". So, the verse implies that the church will be completely separated from the wrath that is to come.

In Luke 21:36, Jesus said "Watch ye therefore, and pray always, that ye may be accounted worthy to escape all these things that shall come to pass, and to stand before the Son of man." Paul writing to the church in Thessalonica said, "and to wait for this Son from heaven, whom he raised from the dead, even Jesus, which delivered us from the wrath to come" (1 Thessalonians 1:10). In 1 Thessalonians 5:9-10 "For God hath not appointed us to wrath, but to obtain salvation by our Lord Jesus Christ, Who died for us, that, whether we wake or sleep, we should live together with him."

The church is absent from all the passages that teaches about the Great tribulation, both in the Old and New Testament (Daniel 8:24-27, 12:1-2, 2 Thess. 2:1-11, Revelation 4-18). The principle of God protecting His people before judgment is clearly seen through the pages of

Scripture. For example, before the Great Flood, God ensured that Noah the righteous and his family were safe in the ark. Lot was delivered from Sodom and Gomorrah before God rained down judgement on that wicked city. Enoch was translated to heaven before the Great Flood came upon the earth. Just like these examples of old, we can rest assured that God will secure the safety of His people, the church, before the judgement of God falls during the period called the great tribulation.

7. Does the implementation of 5G Technology have any connection with the Mark of the Beast?

It is a fact that Technology is transforming the way we do things today. Everything and everyone seems to rely on technology in some way or form, but this was foretold by Daniel the prophet who said that in the last days "many shall run to and fro, and knowledge shall be increased." We see the technology at work because today millions of people are able to fly across the globe, reaching destinations that would have taken them months and even years to reach. Also, we are able to communicate in matter of seconds with people who are living on the other side of the earth through fast telecommunication networks.

This brings me to the question about 5G. Like all the other technologies that have come about recently, 5G is just another one in the scheme of things. It is a massive upgrade to its predecessors i.e. (1G to 4G) and it is simply a technology that allows us to wirelessly communicate and connect everyone and everything together with improved efficiency, more reliability with a greater network capacity and availability. This Technology along with many others will assist the Antichrist to accomplish his goal of a cashless society. But the real question is,

"Is this the actual Mark of the Beast?" My answer to that is "No".

The Mark of the Beast, as described in Revelation 13:11-18, is a mark that will create an allegiance to the Antichrist, but this will be separate and distinct from all the technology used to enable him to enforce his economic system.

8. Have all the prophecies concerning the Messiah been fulfilled?

No, absolutely not! The Bible says there are two kinds of prophecies regarding the Messiah – the prophecies concerning His suffering and those concerning His glory – 1 Peter 1:11. Only the prophecies concerning His suffering have been fulfilled. The prophecies concerning His glory will be fulfilled at the time of His second coming. Read Isaiah 24:21-23 and 2 Thess. 1:10.

9. Does the Nation of Israel play a role in end-time prophecy?

Israel will play a great role in end-time prophecy. In reality, it can be argued that Israel is the centre and time clock of Bible Prophecy. Daniel, in talking about the end of days, declares that the prophecy of the seventy weeks is determined to his people (Israel) and to his city (Judah) (See Daniel 9:24). In fact, the whole story in Bible prophecy is unfolded in and around Israel, and every major event points back to that little piece of land in the Middle East, the city of Jerusalem.

In 1948 we see Israel being reborn as nation and this was after being in exile in other nations for many years. This had to happen as God did prophesy to them that He will take them from among the nations, gather them out of all countries, and bring them into their own land (Ezekiel 36:24).

God also made them a promise that they will become prosperous and will never again suffer the disgrace of famine among the nations (Ezekiel 36:30). This single event in 1948 is necessary, because in order for all the other forthcoming prophecies to make sense, Israel has to exist as a nation. For example, it is with Israel that the Antichrist will make an agreement at the beginning of the great tribulation (Daniel 9:27), and he will break the covenant in the middle of the tribulation (Daniel 9:27).

In Revelation 7:4 the Antichrist will seek to annihilate the whole nation of Israel, but God is going to seal them (Revelation 7:4) and offer protection and nourishment in the wilderness for a time, and times, and half a time, that is three and a half years (Revelation 12: 14). At the battle of Armageddon, we see Jesus returning with the saints and He will devour the Antichrist and all those that came up against Israel (Revelation 20:7-9). This great event will cause Israel to be fully persuaded that Jesus is their Messiah who has returned to deliver them (Zechariah 12:10, Matthew 23:37,

Isaiah 53:1-9) and they will be converted (Zechariah 12:2-13:1). After this we see Israel again, finally possessing the Promised Land in the Millennial Kingdom and Jesus Christ will sit on the throne of David (1 Chronicles 17:11–14, 2 Chronicles 6:16, 2 Samuel 7) to reign on this earth as King of kings and Lord of lords.

10. When will Judgements Take Place?

The Bible highlights five major judgments that will take place, one is in the past and the other four are in the future. The five judgements are (1) the Judgement of sin at Calvary, (2) the Judgement of the Great Tribulation, (3) the Judgement Seat of Christ, (4) the Judgement of the Nations, and (5) the Great White Throne Judgement.

Now, when will these judgements take place? The first Judgement took place at the cross in Jerusalem where Jesus died for the sins of the whole world. It was at Calvary that Jesus took the wrath that we all deserved – 2 Cor 5:21. The Apostle Peter said "Who His own self bare our sins in His own body on the tree, that we, being dead to sins, should live unto righteousness." 1 Pet. 2:24.

The second Judgement will take place in the future, during the time called the Great Tribulation or the "time of Jacob's trouble" – Daniel 12:1 and Jeremiah 30:7. At this judgement God is going to cause Israel to "pass under the rod." Ezekiel 20:34-36 and to be cast into God's "Melting Pot" (Ezekiel 22:19-21).

The third Judgement is also futuristic, but this will not be on the earth, but it will take place in heaven, after the rapture. At this judgement, the church will "appear before the 'Judgment Seat of Christ" to give an account of the works done in our body while we were on earth – 2 Cor 5:10. It must be noted that all who appear before the judgement seat of Christ will be saved and as such they will not be judged for sin, but for their works, in order to determine their degrees of reward. Every work done by the Christian will be tried with fire and if they are bad works as represented by wood, hay and stubble they will be consumed but if our works are gold, silver or precious stones then the fire will only purify it and we will be rewarded for it (see 1 Cor 3: 9-13).

The fourth Judgement is called the Judgement of the Nations, which will take place after the Great Tribulation and right before the Millennium on the earth in the valley of Jehoshaphat (Joel 3: 1-3, Matt. 25:31-46.). All nations, excluding Israel and the church, will be judged. Those nations that treated Israel well will be considered the sheep nations and those who fought against Israel will be the goat nations (Matthew 25: 32-33). The sheep nations will live on after the great Tribulation into the Millennium and some will even inherit the new earth to live eternally (Revelation 21:24, St. Matthew 25:46) but the goat nations will not make it into the

Millennium. They will be cursed and cast into eternal fire (Matthew 25:41).

The fifth and final Judgement will be for the unsaved. Their judgement will occur at the end of the Millennium on the earth at the Great White Throne. This judgement will be for all ungodly from the beginning of time (2 Peter 3:7) and they will be judged out of the book of life. All who find themselves before this judgement will not be saved but will forever be cast into the lake of fire (Read Revelation 20:11-15).

11. **Does Russia play any role in end-time prophecy?**

Yes. Ezekiel prophesied that there will be an invasion of Israel by massive forces of which Russia will be apart. The goal of Russia and its companions will be to utterly wipe out the Jews (Ezekiel 36-37) This invasion is believed by many bible prophecy scholars to be right after the rapture, because of the confusion it will cause in the world Russia will seize the moment to invade Israel. But, this invasion will be short lived because (1) it is a direct challenge to the Antichrist who will sign a covenant with Israel

(Daniel 9:27) and (2) God is going to supernaturally destroy the invading forces on the hills of Israel (Ezekiel 39). Read Ezekiel 38 & 39.

12. Will We Know Each Other in Heaven?

Yes, definitely. We are told that we will have glorified bodies like the one that Jesus had after his resurrection – Phillipians 3:21. Once the disciples got over the shock of His resurrection, they easily recognized Him whenever He appeared to them - John 21:7. In like manner, the disciples recognized Moses and Elijah when they appeared at the transfiguration of Jesus - Matthew 17:1-5. We do not become non-entities at death. We retain our individuality and personality. God constantly refers to Himself as "the God of Abraham, Isaac and Jacob" long after their deaths. His fellowship with them is obviously continuing in Heaven. See Luke 20:37-38.

GLOSSARY

AIDS-- Acquired Immuno-Deficiency Syndrome

BPO—Business Process Outsourcing

BSE— Bovine spongiform encephalopathy

EU—European Union

ISIS—Islamic State of Iraq and Syria

NATO—North Atlantic Treaty Organization

NFC—Near Field Communication

RFID— Radio-Frequency-Identification

SARS—Severe Acute Respiratory Syndrome

SEZ—Special Economic Zone

TRN—Tax-Payer Registration Number

UK—United Kingdom

UN—United Nations

US/ USA—United States of America

USSR— Union of Soviet Socialist Republics

WFH—Work From Home

BIBLIOGRAPHY

Cool, Terry L. **The Mark of the New World Order.** Whittaker House, 1996

CVM Television. *Beyond the Crisis: Road to Recovery* Sunday, July 5, 2020

Hagee, John. **Beginning of the End.** Thomas Nelson Publishers, 1996

Johnson, Larry. **The Last Days of Planet Earth.** Harvest House Publishers, 1991

Lewis, David A. **Magog 1982: Cancelled.** New Leaf Press, 1982

Lindsay, Hal. **The Late Great Planet Earth.** Zondervan Publishing House, 1970

Mers, Texe, Tim LaHaye, *et al* **Storming Toward Armageddon: Essays in Apocalypse** New Leaf Press, 1996

Pentecost, Dwight. **Things to Come.** Dunham, 1958

Scofield, C. I. **The Scofield Reference Bible.** Oxford University, 1909

Websites/ Articles

Beaumont, Peter. *"Millions hang by a thread': extreme global hunger compounded by Covid-19"* in Global Development in **The Guardian,** Tue 21 Apr 2020 (Retrieved April 28, 2020) https://www.theguardian.com/global-development/2020/apr/21/millions-hang-by-a-thread-extreme-global-hunger-compounded-by-covid-19-coronavirus

Christians Together. *"EU architect would welcome God or the Devil"* July 15, 2012 https://www.christianstogether.net/Articles/319656/Christians_Together_in/Christian_Life/Christians_and_Politics/EU_architect_would.aspx

Gerard O'Connell. *Pope Francis to world's religious leaders: We build the future together or there will be no future* in **America: The Jesuit Review.** February 04, 2019
https://www.americamagazine.org/faith/2019/02/04/

pope-francis-worlds-religious-leaders-we-build-

future-together-or-there-will-be-no

Gyatso, Tenzin. *Many Faiths, One Truth* in Opinion in **The New York Times** May 24, 2010
https://www.nytimes.com/2010/05/25/opinion/25gyatso.html

Dahir, A bdi Latif. *"Instead of Coronavirus, the Hunger Will Kill Us.' A Global Food Crisis Looms."* in **The New York Times** April 22, 2020 (Retrieved April 28, 2020)
https://nyti.ms/3eHELic

Elliot, Larry. *"Gordon Brown calls for global government to tackle coronavirus"* in Politics in **The Guardian** Thu 26 Mar 2020 (Retrieved April 28, 2020)
https://www.theguardian.com/politics/2020/mar/26/gordon-brown-calls-for-global-government-to-tackle-coronavirus

Francis, Kimone. *"Some Jamaicans returning home must consent to geofencing"* in **The Jamaica Observer,** Tuesday, May 19, 2020 (Retrieved July 5, 2020)
http://www.jamaicaobserver.com/news/some-jamaicans-returning-home-must-consent-to-geofencing_194453?profile=1373

Graham-Laird, Narda G. *A Legal Introduction to Jamaica's SEZ Regime* **DunnCox** June 2, 2019
https://www.lexology.com/library/detail.aspx?g=4a7c07d4-42b3-49df-aff4-131c103acee8

Harper, Jim. *The New National Identification Systems.* **Cato Institute**, Policy Analysis No. 831, January 30, 2018
https://www.cato.org/publications/policy-analysis/new-national-id-systems

Hewitt-Coleman, Tim."*Towards one world, one government"* Opinion in **The Herald,** 15 April 2020 (Retrieved April 28, 2020)
https://www.heraldlive.co.za/opinion/2020-04-15-towards-one-world-one-government/

Kang Jin-kyu. *North Korea blows up inter-Korean liaison office near border with South,* AFP in News in **Barron's** June 16, 2020 (Retrieved June 17, 2020) https://www.barrons.com/news/north-korea-blows-up-inter-korean-liaison-office-near-border-with-south-01592293205

Muller, Robert. **World Business Academy: Global Reconstruction**, September 29, 2005, Vol. 19, Issue 8, *Proper Earth Government: A framework and ways to create it*
https://search.archives.un.org/uploads/r/united-nations-archives/5/9/0/5900c127687eb20ba587e17b8906da66c533a663f68fe5a41c980232fb656d30/S-1100-0004-21-00003.pdf

OSHO. **Towards the Unknown.** Diamond Pocket Books (P) Ltd., New Delhi, 2005
https://books.google.com.jm/books?id=zN_KiXLgmVgC&pg=PA125&lpg=PA125&dq

Oxfam International. *"Hungry in a world of plenty: millions on the brink of famine"* (Retrieved April 27, 2020)
https://www.oxfam.org/en/hungry-world-plenty-millions-brink-famine

Patterson, Chris. *"Revised NIDS Bill To Be Considered by Cabinet Soon"* April 30, 2020
https://jis.gov.jm/revised-nids-bill-to-be-considered-by-cabinet-soon/

Schwartz, Oscar. *The rise of microchipping: are we ready for technology to get under the skin?* **The Guardian.** November 8, 2019 (https://www.theguardian.com/technology/2019/nov/08/the-rise-of-microchipping-are-we-ready-for-technology-to-get-under-the-skin)

Shin, Hyonhee and Josh Smith *"North Korea destroys inter-Korean liaison office in 'terrific explosion"* in **Reuters** June 15, 2020, (Retrieved July 2, 2020) https://www.reuters.com/article/us-northkorea-southkorea/north-korea-destroys-inter-korean-liaison-office-in-terrific-explosion-idUSKBN23M31Q

Twelde, Michael. *"As famines of 'biblical proportion' loom, Security Council urged to 'act fast"* in Humanitarian Aid in **UN News** (Retrieved April 27, 2020)

https://news.un.org/en/story/2020/04/1062272#

van der Merwe, Jewel. *The Latter Rain* in **Discernment Newsletter** Issue # 9, Volume #4, August/ September 1998

http://www.discernment-ministries.com/Newsletters/NL1998JulAug.pdf

5G Technology (Retrieved July 4, 2020)

https://www.qualcomm.com/invention/5g/what-is-5g

http://www.emfexplained.info/?ID=25916

National Identification System (NIDS) (Retrieved July 4, 2020)

https://opm.gov.jm/portfolios/national-identification-system/

RFID Micro-chip

Everything you need to know before getting an RFID implant. https://medicalfuturist.com/rfid-implant-chip/

Tax-Payer Registration Number

https://www.jamaicatax-online.gov.jm/Portal/tax_faqs.html

Image Credits

US Dollar Bill
https://st2.depositphotos.com/4225551/6582/i/950/depositphotos_65823651-stock-photo-one-us-dollar-banknote-back.jpg

www.ingramcontent.com/pod-product-compliance
Lightning Source LLC
Chambersburg PA
CBHW050803160426
43192CB00010B/1626